Understanding

Latin Americans

OTHER BOOKS BY THE SAME AUTHOR
also available from the William Carey Library

God's Word in Man's Language

Message and Mission: The Communication

of the Christian Faith

Customs and Cultures

Understanding
Latin Americans

WITH SPECIAL REFERENCE TO
RELIGIOUS VALUES AND MOVEMENTS

Eugene A. Nida

William Carey Library

SOUTH PASADENA, CALIF.

Copyright © 1974 by Eugene A. Nida
All Rights Reserved

No part of this book may be used or reproduced in any
manner whatsoever without written permission except in
the case of brief quotations embodied in critical articles
and reviews.

Library of Congress Cataloging in Publication Data

Nida, Eugene Albert, 1914-
  Understanding Latin Americans.

  Published in 1969 under title: Communications
of the Gospel in Latin America.
  Bibliography: p.
  1. National characteristics, Latin American.
2. Latin America--Religion. I. Title
F1408.3.N52 1974   301.29's   73-80164
ISBN 0-87808-117-8

In accord with some of the most recent thinking in the aca-
demic press, the William Carey Library is pleased to present
this scholarly book which has been prepared from an author-
edited and author-prepared camera-ready manuscript.

Published by the William Carey Library
533 Hermosa Street
South Pasadena, Calif. 91030
TEL. 213-682-2047

Contents

50818

Preface

This volume is a revised edition of *Communication of the Gospel in Latin America*, which appeared as No. 53 in the series *Sondeos*, published by Centro Intercultural de Documentación (CIDOC). In view of certain significant revisions of detail, the omission of one chapter, and the rearrangement of the material, a new title seems to be desirable. The present title and subtitle (*Understanding Latin Americans: with special reference to religious values and movements*) will, I believe, reveal more accurately the purpose and contents of the book.

Part I consists of an analysis of basic Latin personality characteristics, as described primarily by Latin psychologists and essayists, which can readily be seen from the footnotes and bibliography. Part II explores four aspects of the background and developments of the religious life of Latin America, with special reference to movements within Protestantism.

The chapters of Part II were published in an earlier form in *Practical Anthropology*, a journal dedicated to the application of anthropological insights to the problems of missionary activity. The material of Part I is scheduled to appear in some forthcoming numbers of the same journal.

The chapters of this volume were written before the important developments in the Roman Catholic Church associated with Pope John XXIII and Vatican II. Accordingly, they do not reflect certain very significant changes which have taken place in (1) ecumenical understanding, (2) greatly increased social concern on the part of the Roman Catholic Church, and (3) the biblical renewal, which has stimulated much greater interest in the message of the Bible and the proclamation of the Good News in Roman Catholic churches.

As will be clearly evident to the reader, much of what is described in this volume and many of the insights noted are applicable more to Mexico and Guatemala than to the rest of Latin America. There are two reasons for this. First, the author has much greater personal acquaintance with these two countries than with other regions and quite naturally he draws considerably upon his own background. Second, Mexican psychologists, psychiatrists, and philosophers have been much more prone to discuss and analyze Hispanoamerican traits than have those in other regions of the Latin world. Accordingly, bibliographical sources and data tend to reflect primarily certain features of Mexican life. However, there are very clear parallels to other parts of the Hispanoamerican world; and though the applications may not be direct, the analogies are sufficiently clear to provide helpful insights into problems in other regions.

For important critical judgments and advice on a number of points in the analysis of the themes in Latin American life, I am deeply indebted to a number of my colleagues: Gonzalo Báez-Camargo, Jacob A. Loewen, Ivan Nothdurft, Alfredo Tépox V., and William L. Wonderly.

Greenwich, Connecticut
January 1974   EUGENE A. NIDA

Part I

Major Themes
in Latin American Life

1
Similarities and Contrasts

In comparison with the dramatic contrasts between the
Orient and the Western World, between Negro Africa and
industrialized Europe, and between the masses of India and
the rural population of North America, the differences
between the Latin American and North American ways of
life seem minimal; and yet underlying these apparent
similarities are many significant contrasts, which from
time to time cause serious misunderstanding and tragic
failures in comprehension. Too often people in the Americas
rather blindly assume that they are all alike. Do they not
share a common cultural background in Europe? Are
they not bound by links of a common Christendom? Are
they not similarly new nations in the New World? But
these apparent similarities only tend to mask certain
basic differences which, if unrecognized, contribute to
continued mutual suspicion and even hostility.

Orientals and Africans are so obviously different that
North Americans expect their ways of life to be radically
diverse. Therefore they are not surprised when there are
failures of comprehension. But in the Western Hemisphere
most North Americans expect similarities, when in reality
there are radical diversities; and they assume understanding, when in actuality people are often talking on quite
different wavelengths.

To many North Americans, people of Latin America seem strangely contradictory: so passionate and yet so melancholy; so dedicated to the joys of life but so cynical about the chances for happiness; so much in love with life but so preoccupied with symbols of death; so colorful (in dress, fiesta, or politics) but so depressed in slums, poverty, and revolution. On the other hand, to the average Latin American most North Americans seem to be predictably materialistic, banal, and "flat"—as tasteless as a meal served in an automat.

Even within the areas of church life there are radical differences between North America and Latin America. Maryknoll Fathers have been run out of Guatemalan towns for denouncing pagan practices which had been hallowed by time and patiently tolerated by a local clergy. Protestants have thought that mission-founded churches in Latin America would function more or less as their North American models, only to discover that constitutions mean very little when there is a clash of strong personalities in the church. Just as some countries do not obtain a new president without a revolution, so some churches do not "elect" a new pastor without a similarly ruinous struggle for power within the church.

North American Roman Catholics are often shocked to discover that some of the most dynamic persons in the Roman Catholic movement in Latin America are convinced and dedicated socialists—bent on violent revolution as the only way of bringing justice to a much abused people. Protestants in North America are equally bewildered to see that although their own missionary programs are beginning to "level off" in growth and influence, numerous indigenous Protestant movements are growing with incredible dynamic force and power. In Chile such movements, though receiving absolutely no help from abroad, are four times the size of all mission-sponsored churches. In Mexico there are four principal indigenous churches which have been in existence for only about 30 years but which even now have as many members as all the traditional Protestant churches in the country.

These distinctively national movements in Latin America, whether Roman Catholic or Protestant, are quite different in structure, ethos, manner of communication, and message from the foreign imposed programs originating abroad. And yet these movements do have some strikingly similar features, reflecting a number of important aspects of Latin personality. It is for this reason that anyone who would understand the dynamic developments in Latin America must gain some basic insight into those fundamental drives and themes of life which may be said to explain why Latins "tick." To study such matters, however, one must limit the scope of analysis and set up some bases for contrast and comparison.

The scope of this study

It should be clearly evident that if we are to study the Latin way of life, especially in relationship to basic features of Latin personality, both our study and our approach must be restricted. To take in all of Latin America would be quite impossible, for when we speak of Latin America as a whole, we are talking about an area which surpassed North America in population in the 1950s and is expected to have twice as many people as North America by the year 2000.[1] Its principal languages are Spanish and Portuguese, but some people speak English (many areas of the Caribbean), French (Haiti), and Dutch (Dutch Antilles), as well as some 250 indigenous Indian tongues. The racial composition of different countries in Latin America also differs widely. In Bolivia and Guatemala more than 50 percent of the population is Indian, while in Costa Rica, Chile, Uruguay, Colombia, Venezuela, and Argentina, the population is predominately white. In most other countries in Latin America the dominant population is largely mestizo (Indian and White), but in some countries there is a very considerable mulatto population (e.g. Cuba and the Dominican Republic). In economic development the countries of Latin America also differ enormously, with Mexico having a number of modern industrialized centers while Paraguay remains largely agricultural. In terms of cultural orientation the Latin countries are also quite different. Mexico is proudly and rightly mestizo, but Uruguay is predominantly Europe-oriented. Venezuela has had a long tradition of authoritarianism (strong dictators) in its political life but has been largely democratic in its

social outlook—something made possible by its long tradition of public schools. On the other hand, Colombia has
had a rather liberal political life, but in its social structures
it has been quite hierarchical.

Some countries of Latin America are in the process of
profound and rapid social change:[2] regionalism is giving
way to nationalism; nationalism is developing distinct forms
in all the various countries; agriculture is ceding to
industrialization; people from rural areas are moving at
alarming rates into the sprawling capitals (Mexico City is
now as large as Chicago).

Due to the complexity and extent of Latin America, this
study is limited essentially to the Spanish-speaking
countries, thus excluding, for example, Haiti, which poses
very special problems due to the dominance of many West
African traits, and Brazil, which, though sharing in many
Iberian traits, exhibits some very important differences
from Spanish-speaking Latin America. For one thing,
there is considerable West African influence in Brazilian
life. There is also a much longer and more liberal tradition
in Brazil, for the Inquisition was never as strong in that
land as it was in Spanish-speaking Latin America. Furthermore, there is a rather special development of spiritism
in Brazil (involving an estimated 10 million persons),
which, though paralleled by some similar movements
in other areas of Latin America, has a number of distinctive features that make it a subject requiring particular
and separate attention.

Furthermore, this analysis does not attempt to deal with
the Indian population of Latin America, which numbers some
15 million people who are distinctive in dress, language,
and patterns of association.[3] Even the bilingual Indians, of
which there are several million, have not taken on distinctive Hispanoamerican features of personality, and their
value systems are quite different from those of Latins
generally, although the Indians, especially in Mexico, have
seemingly had a rather significant influence on certain
Hispanoamerican traits. By way of contrast with Latins,
certain special features of Indian ways will be discussed in
Chapter 4, but no attempt is made to carry out a systematic
study of the contrasts. It is most important, however, that
one distinguish between the Indian way of life and the type of

behavior of those who may simply speak an Indian language. For example, except for about 50,000 persons, all Paraguayans speak Guaraní, an indigenous language of South America, and at least 500,000 Paraguayans speak only Guaraní. This does not mean, however, that they are Indian in either their outlook or their background. The culture of these people is essentially Spanish, and their value systems are distinctively Latin.

We also exclude from this study the large English-speaking Negro populations of the Caribbean region, for in terms of manner of life and value systems they do not fit within the Hispanoamerican framework. Many thousands of these people are, however, being rapidly assimilated into the Spanish-speaking communities of their respective countries, e.g. Panama, Nicaragua, and Costa Rica, and they are gradually assimilating distinctive Latin values and orientations.

As will be noted in the following sections, special emphasis has been placed in Part I on developments in Mexico. There are several reasons for this: (1) sociological and psychological analyses have been carried out more extensively by Mexican scholars; (2) antithetical contrasts, typical of Latin American life generally, are most acutely accentuated in Mexico (thus providing a framework within which more subtle differences in other areas may be judged and evaluated); (3) the contrasts between Latin Americans and North Americans (certain cultural comparisons are both essential and illuminating) are most striking in the context of Mexican versus Yankee (or Gringo) values; and (4) the author has much greater experience and personal acquaintance with the situation in Mexico than with any other area in Latin America. Nevertheless, despite this frequent focus of attention upon Mexico, the student of Latin America will constantly see the broader application of the observations and insights.

Levels of similarity and contrast

Faced with such a seemingly bewildering array of differences in Latin America, even within the scope which has been left for this analysis, one might think that finding basic similarities or contrasts would be hopelessly complicated. However, the finding of such similarities and contrasts is very largely a matter of the level of analysis. The typical tourist is, of course, impressed with the similarities in so many parts of Latin America: the tile roofs, central plazas, imposing colonnades, colorful dances, folk music, Spanish language, systems of gestures, and patterns of courtesy. On the other hand, if this same tourist lives in various parts of Latin America for a time, he becomes aware of a deeper level of distinctiveness, for the dream of the liberator Simón Bolívar for hemispheric Latin unity was never realized. Rather, with political independence came greater fragmentizing of power under strong local *caudillos*, who to a degree led Latin America back into a kind of medieval feudalism. These diverse historical developments help to explain the contrasts between a quiet, peaceful Costa Rica, which has boasted more schoolhouses than soldiers, and a revolutionary Mexico, in which there is an incredibly high rate of murders of passion, and in which Pancho Villa is still a popular idol. Diverse historical traditions help to explain how Uruguay and Argentina, which in the 19th century looked so much to France as a model, are so different from Colombia, which was more thoroughly steeped in Spanish ways. Even within individual countries there are striking contrasts. Colombia's Medellín is staunchly conservative, while Barranquilla has been traditionally liberal. Similarly, Ecuador's Guayaquil has spawned a host of liberal revolutions, while Quito has remained the fortress of traditional and conservative ways. Within all Latin countries a wide cleavage has separated the rich and the poor. But now all of Latin America is experiencing a rising middle class of technicians and operators, whose control of the functions of society is putting them increasingly into places of dominance.

Values in Latin society and personality

The careful student of Latin America sees below the surface of the differences in Latin patterns of life and dis-covers very important similarities, for despite the diverse ways in the Latin world, there are many shared values which help to explain the essential similarities in outlook and practice. These values have been variously analyzed, but the following is a typical listing:[4] personal dignity, kinship ties, stratification of society, materialism (of a distinctive kind), spiritual values, value of the inner state (espiritualidad), emotional expression, fatalism, a decent way of life, opposition to manual labor.[5]

Samuel Ramos, distinguished professor of philosophy of the University of Mexico, characterizes Latin personality in terms of certain basic psychological characteristics: distrust, resulting in a sense of inferiority and pessimism; resentment of criticism, with a marked tendency to react defensively and to quarrel; passion; aggression. Ramos insists that the combination of distrust and sensitivity to criticism compels many Latins to convince themselves constantly that others are inferior.[6]

María Elvira Bermúdez,[7] outstanding Mexican psychiatrist, presents a somewhat similar analysis of Latin personality traits: inferiority complex, resentment, irresponsibility, contradictory tendencies. As will be noted, the first two traits correspond closely with what Samuel Ramos has noted. Perhaps, however, one of the most important insights of Dr. Bermúdez is this indication of "contradictory tendencies," for this is precisely what one finds in the values listed by John P. Gillin and Lyman Bryson. Compare, for example, such contrasts as materialism and spiritual values, spirituality and fatalism, a decent way of life and opposition to manual labor, personal dignity and emotional expression. Some aspects of these values certainly seem to be contradictory.

Rogelio Díaz Guerrero, psychiatrist and professor in the University of the Americas, Mexico City, has made a very careful study of the values of a particular class of Mexican people, namely, the working class, and for these persons he discovered that the major values were sexual capacity, money, friendship, personal dignity, recreation or amusement.[8] Here again there seems to be something disparate in rating money and friendship as almost equally high in the esteem of the people. It is evident that such features do not easily go together. What is needed is some framework which can explain how such seemingly diverse values can be combined into some structured whole, for people do not respond to mere lists of disparate values. In some way or other such values must constitute a workable system which provides a rationale for the seeming discrepancies and a basis for choice between contradictory or competing values.

One must recognize, of course, that social values and psychological characteristics are not the same for all persons in any society. In fact, within a single society there are usually greater differences than there are between the norms of different societies. Nevertheless, there is some truth in the concept of norms and of predominantly shared values, for these are the features which do help to explain the differences between societies and to give them their distinctive "flavor."

Anthropologists have long recognized that significant differences exist between nations as well as between individuals. Certainly the values of the average Mexican laborer are not identical with those of laborers in Costa Rica, for the histories of these two nations are quite distinct and their traditions are markedly diverse. Nevertheless, within any so-called culture area there are certain shared elements, which in a greater or lesser degree characterize its life and thus help to explain the distinctive features of life in such areas as North America, Latin America, Japan, the South Pacific, and West Africa.

It is very important to note that the basic personality characteristics introduced here and discussed in subsequent chapters come from leading authorities in the field, most of whom are Latins themselves (see Bibliography). Basically this treatment depends for its insights on the writings of Miguel de Unamuno (who has written of Latin personality with most unusual depth of understanding), Samuel Ramos, Santiago Ramírez, Octavio Paz, Aniceto Aramoni, and María Elvira Bermúdez. It is interesting that all but one of these persons are Mexicans. Any examination of the critical and scientific literature on evaluations of Latin personality clearly shows that Mexicans have investigated this field most widely and have published their observations most fully. In some measure, at least, this is due to the fact that, more than any other Latins, Mexicans may be said to have "found themselves." Therefore they can most readily be self-critical.

This analysis does not include any observations not already noted by Latins themselves. It is not a new description of Latin values but an attempt to place these various values and characteristics into some meaningful structure which will show the dynamic relationships between the competing parts. In other words, this is not an attempt to make any fresh observations of the field but rather to obtain some new insights into matters which Latins themselves have carefully explored and expertly described. In order to do this, we must obviously omit some features of detail, for we cannot obtain the broad perspective if we concentrate unduly on the details. We would then not be able to see the forest because of the trees. Moreover, we are not attempting to treat the historical factors which have produced these features of personality or sets of values, for we are concerned with the dynamic interaction and behavior of people, not with the historical reasons for such developments.

Structured contrasts

A careful study of the various value systems and personality traits of Latin America reveals three major sets of contrasting features which seem to provide the dynamic structure for the evaluation and patterning of Latin behavior. These contrasts may be called: (1) authoritarianism versus individualism (*personalismo*), (2) idealism (*quijotismo*) versus realism (*sanchismo*), and (3) *machismo* versus *hembrismo*. It is unfortunate that one cannot find fully adequate English equivalents for *quijotismo, sanchismo, machismo,* and *hembrismo*. No translation does complete justice to the special values associated with these words. Essentially, of course, *quijotismo* refers to the kind of romantic idealism associated with Cervantes' famous character Don Quijote, and *sanchismo* identifies the opposite earthy and materialistic concern for immediate physical gratification so characteristic of Don Quijote's constant companion, Sancho Panza[9]. *Machismo* is a term for male dominance, but it also signifies male sexuality, authoritarianism, and display. *Hembrismo*, on the contrary, denotes female dependence, passivity, and receptivity.

On the basis of Unamuno's insight into the dualistic spirit in Latin personality, which polarizes the contrasts into opposing sets[10], these three basic sets of values have been selected since they seem to give meaning to the other traits. Life is thus not regarded as a series of traits or as a string of habits but as a structured whole, a system of interrelated parts, which in their functioning intersect with each other and provide the familiar polychromatic character of Latin life. It is only by appreciating the functioning of such contradictory traits, which remain in constant tension with one another, that some of the contradictory features of Latin behavior can be understood.

Only by this means can one comprehend how a man is willing one day to risk his life for the sake of freedom and on the following, as the victorious dictator, to tramp out all vestiges of freedom. Similarly, we can understand better how a bitterly anticlerical person can still keep an image of the Virgin in his bedroom, and how a lover of democracy and freedom could collaborate with the Nazis during World War II in order to try to bring about the defeat of the United States.

By possessing such contradictory tendencies, Latin life has always been "colorful," even though it may have frequently been dangerously chaotic. But this is the way Latins prefer life. They are proud of their "Golden Age," but they would never opt for a "golden mean," for this would produce the kind of mechanical efficiency of well-ordered mediocrity regarded as being the essence of Yankee imperialism. Hence the Latin, as Unamuno and others have so effectively shown, combines constantly the twin images of the idealist Don Quijote and the realist Sancho Panza. This does not mean that in every action each Latin is a behavioral schizophrenic—split between opposite values and governed by thoroughly contradictory values—but it does mean that there is a constant fluctuation between opposite extremes. Hence, the same person may be a fanatical idealist in politics but a very sensuous realist in sex. He may offer his life to defend justice but use his money to pervert judges. He will defend to the death the virginity of his sister but not hesitate to destroy the virginity of a woman "whose heart he has conquered in courtship."

In order to avoid subjectivity and circularity in the analysis of cultural traits, it is essential to have some basis of comparison, and it is for this reason that we can perhaps most meaningfully compare Latin life with North

American life. We could just as easily make such comparisons with patterns of life in Japan, Malaysia, or East Africa, but for our practical purposes the contrast with North American life is more meaningful and appropriate. Some of the most interesting analyses of such differences have already been made by Latins themselves. Octavio Paz,[11] for example, has listed a number of contrasting features which seem to him to be highly significant. He contends that the Latin will lie readily for the sake of fantasy or to overcome a sordid life, whereas the North American will frequently insist on telling the truth. The Latin gets drunk in order to confess, whereas the North American gets drunk to forget. The Latin is basically nihilistic, whereas the North American is an optimist. The Latin is often distrustful and suspicious, whereas the North American is more open. The Latin prefers to "contemplate," whereas the North American insists on "understanding." Finally, the Latin is a revolutionary, bent on radical change, whereas the North American is more interested in reform and improvement. Samuel Ramos[12] adds that one of the important distinctions is that the Latin came to the New World to exploit it, and the North American came to populate it. A still further contrast, pointed out by Luis Quintanilla,[13] is that the Latin came to transplant the Old World while the North American came to create a New World.

Though many of these contrasts pointed out by Latins seem to be unfavorable to Latins, there are other contrasts which are certainly unfavorable to North Americans and which, perhaps because of politeness, Latins have not mentioned: less capacity of North Americans to enjoy beauty, less concern for the spiritual dimension of life, impatience, program-oriented rather than person-oriented activity, failure to relax, and striving for "success," regardless of consequences to health, family, and associates.

In such comparisons of North Americans and Latins as will be made in this analysis, there is no intention of proving one set of values superior to another but merely of indicating that they are different. Ultimate evaluation is not something which any person as a member of any one society can ever make with complete objectivity. Moreover, individual preferences are largely dependent on personal values rather than on any broad cultural or social formulations. Though, of course, most North Americans presumably prefer their own value systems, many of them, including the present writer, have deep admiration for, and sincere appreciation of, Latin values. In fact, they often feel more at home with Latins than with their own countrymen.

The decision to contrast Latin with North American value systems is dictated by very practical concerns. In the first place, more people have some knowledge of these two systems. Furthermore, the contrasts seem even more significant, since the two cultures share so much: geographical proximity, a European cultural heritage, long interrelationship, and a common link in Christendom, despite the important differences between Protestant and Roman Catholic backgrounds. Moreover, it is hoped that this type of treatment can be mutually helpful to those engaged in continuing communication between Latins and North Americans—a dialogue which must continue and grow.

If we are to speak meaningfully about differences of values, we must deal with them in a wide range of behavior, for no single viewpoint or aspect of life is sufficient to explain fully just what is involved. This means that we must attempt to analyze the outworking of the three basic contrasts on the various levels of Latin life: religious, philosophical, political, aesthetic, social, and familial. In most instances we consider the religious aspects first, since they are so vital to the understanding of Latin life. Samuel Ramos,[14] among others, has rightly insisted that religion is the unifying principle of Latin life, since it has been the principal vehicle of culture transmission through its control of education. However, in describing the contrasts between *machismo* and *hembrismo*, it seems essential to begin with the family, for this is crucial. At each point where it seems relevant, we attempt to point out some of the important similarities and contrasts with North American patterns of life, and then, in a final summary, we deal with some of the contrasts in Indian life.

2
Authoritarianism and Individualism

Authoritarianism stands for a structured control of society from some "top" or "center." The avowed purpose of authoritarian control is unity, and generally the proclaimed basis is some doctrinaire concern for tradition. In any event the society (as expressed in and through its leadership) takes priority over the individual.

Individualísm, on the other hand, may be described as expressing itself primarily in terms of personal reaction and revolt against the status quo, with strong appeals to liberty and a tendency to radicalism (or break with tradition) in politics, religion, and art. By emphasizing the "dignity of the individual" and "his personal rights," opponents of authoritarianism introduce tensions and conflict, both on the national as well as on the family level. In fact, this basic dichotomy in values has profound implications for the entire range of human behavior.

Religion

Before one can understand the significance of authoritarianism and individualism in the religion of Latin America, one must first appreciate some of the traditional features of Latin Roman Catholicism. Dr. María Bermúdez[1] has bluntly stated the basic characteristics of traditional religion as being (1) magic and superstition for the peasant, (2) a matter of convenience for the middle class, and (3) a source of boastful display for the rich. In many instances emphasis on the role of Mary, preoccupation with the function of the saints, a demand for consecrated charms, and an almost morbid preoccupation with symbols of death have left many persons in the Roman Church with only hollow forms. Recently there have been some very significant reform movements within Latin Roman Catholicism. For example, the Bishop of Morelos removed most of the images of the saints from the cathedral and in their place put plaques with Scripture verses. The image of Mary is no longer central to the worship but placed as an "onlooker" to the altar, where the empty cross is the focal symbol. But despite such highly important changes, the Roman clergy in Latin America seems to be losing its hold on the people.[2]

Increasingly many better-educated persons view traditional religion in somewhat the same terms that Santiago Ramirez characterizes it: "Religion—an emblem, a justification, and an excuse for greed."[3] So serious has become the reaction against traditional religion that some persons have pled for a new kind of humanism which will prevent modern secularized man from descending to a "sub-human level."[4]

No doubt part of this strong reaction against institutional religion in Latin America has been the result of a strong authoritarian emphasis. The insistence upon "one faith, one shepherd, one flock—unity above all else" has quite naturally produced a situation in which "dogma is not to be discussed—it can only be accepted or rejected."[5] Accordingly, there have been few, if any, challenging theological developments to keep people in the New World abreast of the new age in which they were living. In fact, in the New World thought control was somewhat greater than in most parts of Western Europe, for the Spanish colonies officially excluded for many years all "Jews, Masons, heretics, and freethinkers."

Part of this insistence on unity is to be understood in terms of the historical developments in Spain, where national unity was attained only by military conquest of the "infidel." This "holy war" produced a kind of brotherhood between the priest and warrior, and certain religious orders were patterned after military organizations.[6] Similarly, military organizations developed quasi-religious goals. Soon victory over the infidels in Spain was reinterpreted as a challenge for *la reconquista de la fe* "the reconquering of the faith" through the Hispanic world.

In view of such emphasis on authoritarianism and unity, it is scarcely any wonder that the compensating tendency of an equally radical individualism also arose. In fact, anticlericalism has been stronger, and often more violent, in Latin America than in any other place in the world.

Within the independence movement in Latin America anticlericalism was especially strong, even among some of the lower clergy; but anticlericalism was even stronger in some of the revolutionary movements which followed, for example, the Mexican Revolution from 1910 to 1917. In the struggles for independence the Masons played an important role, and even today in Latin America military cliques are often strong sources of liberal tendencies.

Such anticlericalism and antichurch sentiments almost always implied severe psychological conflicts for the persons involved, for these individuals generally remained emotionally bound to the church, even though they continued to be unconvinced of its religious message. This often produced a kind of emotional separation between real and ideal values and behavior—fertile ground for the ideas of the freethinkers who were so much influenced by the Encyclopedic movement in 18th-century France.

This conflict between authoritarianism and individualism in the religious life of Latin America meant that in many instances religion implied no great personal involvement. Gonzalo Báez-Camargo[7] has noted this fact in the literature of Latin America, for though writers make considerable use of religious symbols, these are more often than not symbols of affectation or despair. One simply does not find Latin writers dealing meaningfully or extensively with profound religious themes. For the most part, there is a similar lack of deep religious poetry. This has been explained as being in large measure due to relatively little familiarity with the Bible, the intransigence of dogma, and the substitution of visual forms of ritual for the verbal forms of literature and especially poetry.[8] In the emphasis on ritual drama, the worshiper was only the "onlooker." The pageantry never became internalized and hence never sought expression in poetry or song.

This partial vacuum in Latin religious life has been filled in certain instances by what Unamuno has called "pseudo-mysticism," [9] something which seeks the ecstatic joys of illumination beyond the realm of understanding. This may be fine for the intellectually inclined person, but for the masses a much more practical and accessible form of individual religious involvement has been found in spiritism, in which people feel that they are communicating with the souls in the other world and that guidance for this life can be found in the veiled utterances coming from beyond the grave. Somewhat parallel to this type of ecstatic involvement in the spirit world has been the rapid rise of Pentecostalism in Latin America, in which possession by the Holy Spirit has proven even more appealing than contact with the souls of the dead. In both spiritism and Pentecostalism the focus is on the individual, who is no longer the spectator at a drama but is an actor caught up in a whirlwind of ecstasy.

For the average North American this development in Hispanoamerican Christianity is almost impossible to understand. The constitutional provisions for the separation of church and state and the popular feeling that the preacher has no business meddling in politics mean that in North America there have never been the same types of conflicts and tensions. In fact, the results of these diverse patterns of church-state relations have been almost totally different. While in Latin America many people have seen a tendency for the church to swallow up the state, and hence for the society to become "ecclesiastical," in the United States most people see the opposite tendency, for the state to swallow up the church. For this reason they claim that society becomes increasingly secular. Not having experienced the authoritarian demands of the church, North America has never experienced the kind of fanaticism typical of so many situations in Latin America. Nor has there been the tendency to combine a warmly prochurch sentiment with a violently anticlerical reaction. On the other hand, the separation of church and state in the United States has perhaps tended to accelerate indifference on the part of some people and to promote irrelevance on the part of the clergy. It has also made possible a strange anomaly in which some of the most religiously devout persons can also be the most racially and socially bigoted, since the separation of church and state has been interpreted by some to imply a separation of doctrine from life.

The Evangelical churches of Latin America, which probably number some 10 million persons as members, adherents, and "sympathizers," also exhibit some of the same tendencies as are found in traditional Roman Catholicism. The "infallibility of denominational doctrine" is one aspect of the authoritarian principle. But the opposite tendency to individualism also manifests itself in the numerous indigenous denominations or groupings of churches, usually led or dominated by a "strong man." Such leaders often work in almost complete isolation from, if not hostility to, one another. In many countries, the only thing in which all the Protestant forces join is the Bible Society program.

But the Bible Societies often encounter real problems when they undertake revisions of the Scriptures, since many persons cannot see why one should or how one can "change the Bible." Change implies a loss of authority, and for some persons the authority of the words seems to rank even higher than comprehension of the message.

To many Roman Catholics the Evangelical Church seems very strange, and even foreign. This is not merely because the church buildings represent foreign or strange architecture, or because the interiors of the churches seem frighteningly plain, or because the services remind one more of the classroom than of a period of worship. The real differences are much more basic and positive.[10] In the first place, Roman Catholics are often impressed with the centrality of Christ in Evangelical teaching and worship. The absence of images of Mary and the saints in the Evangelical churches reinforces this impression. In the second place, the Evangelical focus is on interior religious experience rather than on exterior forms or symbols of worship. Lastly, the preaching insists on the priority of faith over works and of love over law. These very features are themselves part of the Latin reaction against institutionalized authoritarianism.

Philosophy

It is difficult to discuss religion apart from philosophy or to treat philosophical developments in Latin America apart from parallel movements in religion; but in order to understand the manner in which authoritarianism and individualism are in tension within Latin American life, it is essential to attempt this type of separation. Perhaps the most significant philosophical development in Latin life reflecting the authoritarian principle is the almost constant striving for "total systems." Nothing as partial or incomplete as pragmatism would ever satisfy the typical Latin. Unfortunately, however, the striving for "total systems" has been primarily traditional in orientation. For the most part, Latins are the philosophical descendants of Thomas Aquinas, who may be said to have elevated reason as a means of justifying the status quo or providing a philosophical undergirding to the scholasticism of the Middle Ages. At any rate, the emphasis on authority has been a dominant theme in Latin philosophical writings.

This emphasis has quite naturally extended itself into the realm of education, where too often the practice is for the student to memorize and quote rather than discuss and reason. The typical "lecture" in traditional schools in Latin America is not far removed from its counterpart in the Middle Ages, where because of the shortage of books the professor "read his lecture" so the students could copy it down.

Emphasis on authoritarianism has, however, provided a very fruitful field for exploitation by other totalitarian or authoritarian philosophies, in addition to that of Thomas Aquinas. In the 19th century positivism was quite the vogue, and in Mexico especially it was pressed with the same callous disregard for the individual as any system could have been. A proclivity for authoritarian systems may also help to explain in part the relative popularity of the Chinese brand of Communism in contrast with the Moscow-exported variety, since in addition to advocating a more violent type of overthrow (a radical revolt of the individual against authority), it is also more doctrinaire and more holistic in its approach— hence more congenial to many Latin Americans.

The tendency toward a reactionary individualism in Latin philosophy is relatively weak, for in most instances people have sought total solutions and comprehensive systems, while expressing their individualistic reactions in the political realm. However, one does find in many writers a tendency to individualism in their practice of citing only their own opinions and observations while paying little attention to the studies of others. It is not uncommon for important books to come out without any bibliography. The ideas may have been gleaned from a number of sources, but if the writer is voicing strong oppositon to some institution in society, more likely than not he is entirely preoccupied with his own judgments.

One might even say that at heart many Latins are confirmed "existentialists," though without being aware of the implications of such an epithet. Certainly, existentialism (particularly that of Unamuno) has been very popular in Latin America, since the existential approach to philosophical questions puts man, the individual, at the center of the stage and makes him the focal point of the problem. Latin existentialism can be well described as the individualistic reaction to authoritarian Thomism and positivism, and the fragmentaristic reaction to holism. Here the Latin propensity for intuition and insight, rather than for research and experiment, comes into full play—especially in that form of existentialism which appeals to the violent reactions of those who are in revolt against institutionalized authority.

In the face of insistent demands for a total system and for theoretical rightness, despite practical impossibilities, the average North American becomes thoroughly restive and impatient. He is so convinced that "if it works, it must be all right," that he is quite willing to leave the philosophical justification to others or to a later time. The average North American is simply not interested in grand systems or "God's truth" philosophies. He is quite willing to accept any number of different "solutions," provided they give results. Accordingly, he is much more inclined to accept multiple hypotheses, experiment with these until he finds recurrent patterns of relationships, and then look for some practical application of such knowledge, rather than worry himself about the way in which such concepts or discoveries fit into a comprehensive system. This he is content to leave to the "eggheads" or the "long-hairs." What counts for the North American, therefore, is not philosophy but engineering. He is not interested in the question of "the why of the elephant," but in "bigger and better elephants."

The Evangelical Church in Latin America has, for the most part, not been affected on the philosophical level by these tensions between authoritarianism and individualism, for the level of education has not been such as to involve any high percentage of the Evangelical population in such questions. In general the authoritarian philosophical view has simply been applied to the Bible, and its more or less literal interpretations have been regarded as infallible and fully authoritative. Total exegetical systems (as, for example, in the Scofield Bible) have been appealing to Latins, but these are still largely foreign importations from North America.

However, with the rise of a much more highly educated second and third generation of Evangelical Christians, the philosophical issues within the Protestant community will become increasingly acute, for younger people are no longer satisfied with traditional answers. Moreover, they are insisting on raising issues that their elders are even opposed to discussing, e.g. rights of collective labor, birth control, involvement in politics, and modern psychiatry. These matters are usually discussed quite apart from any overall philosophical system, but they do represent a practical philosophical concern which no longer accepts the authoritarian attitude toward revealed or traditional truth.

Politics

On no level of life is the authoritarian principle more prominent than in the political sphere. According to the authoritarian viewpoint, power must come from the top and be mediated to society through a typical pyramidal structure or governmental hierarchy. Such a power system cannot regard opposition except as treason, for basically in a system in which "error has no rights" there can be neither a two-party system nor "a loyal opposition." Even the toleration of opposition is often regarded as a sign of weakness and a failure in leadership.

Any change of leadership usually involves only a shifting of responsibility among the members of the same ruling class. This means that most so-called revolutions in Latin America have really been very little more than *coups d'état* or changes in the palace guard. The *caudillos* have changed, but the essentially feudal system has remained intact. Even with such changes there are certain fascinating and often tragic failures. One strong leader does not want to complete projects begun by his predecessor. This would be giving too much credit to the ousted leader, and it might also reflect on the creative leadership of the new incumbent. Therefore, everything started by a former regime is wiped out and a new beginning is made.

Part of the authoritarian outlook in political life is no doubt due to the practical problems faced by political leaders of the New World, in which they reflected the struggle for national unity which had taken place in the Iberian peninsula. But a much more meaningful reason for the authoritarian attitude is to be found in the basic belief of many Latin Americans that "men are not born equal." [11] That is to say, they are born lower and higher, as peons and masters, and each man must fulfill his unique gifts by expressing these to the utmost. Therefore, the potential *caudillo* can only be true to himself as he exercises fully his capacity to command. Each commoner needs a *caudillo* in order to fulfill his own potentiality, and similarly the *caudillo* needs his followers if he is to demonstrate his abilities. When this view of social structure is projected on the national scene, it means that the government is the great *patrón*, and it is there that all decisions must ultimately be made. There is plenty of room for local petitions but not for local initiative, because local initiative might rob the leader of his inherent right and obligation to lead.

Within such a system the individual becomes largely lost, especially when he voices opposition or is suspected of disloyal acts, for according to the law he is "guilty until proven innocent." Thus the state (usually as symbolized by some individual person) becomes the ultimate arbiter of rights and roles.

Strange as it may seem, individualism is based on almost the same principle as authoritarianism, only the application is inverted. Individualism insists that all people are not alike. Each man is uniquely different from all others, and as such he possesses a "personal dignity" which must be respected. Each man, therefore, can insist on his personal rights—quite apart from any legal definition of them. Moreover, this insistence not only can but should be backed up by a man's willingness to defend his honor—at any price.

No doubt one important reason for this strong individualism in Latin America is to be found in the 300 years of colonial rule. "Law and order" came to be understood by Latin Americans as an imposition by the oppressors, a tool of domination. Accordingly, disorder and challenging of the law of the state became the duty of every lover of freedom and national independence.

Individuals have also had collective success in defending their rights in revolution, so they have proven that the traditional class structures are not foreordained by God to last forever. But once the victory over an authoritarian institution has been gained, the revolutionaries are very likely to engage in a mad scramble for power, for each individualist looks upon the group as a pedestal for exhibition of his ability to command.

One part of this emphasis on the individual, in contrast with the collective structure, is the focus on the personal leader rather than on the movement. In fact, most revolutions in Latin America have centered on persons, not on ideologies. Even in the Mexican Revolution, which was by far the most ideological of all such movements in Latin America, the rallying points were not so much ideas as persons, and what concepts existed became associated with men, not with movements. Even political parties tend to be considered as expressions of individual personalities more than as representing diverse political platforms. Such attitudes are automatically projected upon other peoples. For example, in Mexico during the Presidential election in which John F. Kennedy and Richard Nixon were competing, the adherents to the respective parties were referred to not as Democrats and Republicans but as *Kennedyistas* and *Nixonianos*.

There are few spheres of life in which the differences between Latin America and North America become clearer than in the realm of politics. North Americans also believe that not all persons are equal, in the sense that some are weak and others are strong, but the weak need to be protected from the strong. Hence there must be a system of checks and balances to guard against totalitarian control. It is not strange that North Americans should have developed this type of system, for many of them left Europe precisely in order to escape from totalitarianism. On the other hand, most Spanish people who came to the New World were intent on extending the royal system, not escaping from it. Hence, to most Latins a system of checks and balances among the executive, legislative, and judicial branches seems not only clumsy and inefficient but even stupid. What right, for example, does the judiciary have to declare invalid a law which has been enacted by leaders "put there by the people"? This would seem to impugn the sovereignty of the people themselves.

A focus on the individual in Latin life has meant that in politics much depends upon friendship, for it is not the law but the interpretation by a person which actually counts.[12] On the contrary, in North America the approach is program-oriented, not person-oriented, and the United States Department of State thinks nothing of rapidly shifting people from one post to another, for it is the program which seems to be all-important, not the people who are supposed to put it into operation.

When Latins are concerned with a change in a program, they are very likely to want to alter it radically—a very understandable reaction to an excessive authoritarianism, which has usually prevented change for a long time. The Latin, therefore, seeks to redeem and remake the world,[13] while the North American is more likely to think in terms of reforming and improving. The Latin will usually rally to the strong leader in order to accomplish such a goal, but the North American will more likely start some local society bent on creating a "ground swell" of opinion which will accomplish the desired goals.

In any rapidly growing Evangelical church in Latin America there are usually strong leaders. Such churches are generally dominated by a pastor, if he is a strong personality, or by some layman, who normally does not take an official position but whose authority is clearly recognized by everyone in the congregation. Such a strong personality is the equivalent of the *dueño* "owner" and the pastor becomes the *mayordomo* "overseer" or "foreman." Many church members have an almost blind faith in the pastor. As one Guatemalan expressed it, "I'm for my pastor, whether he's right or wrong."

But in most instances in which a local leader is too

authoritarian, there is an almost inevitable revolt, especially among the younger members of the congregation. In such a conflict, doctrines are often used as pretexts for denunciations, but the real issues are persons. As the result of such strong differences of opinion, Evangelical churches in Latin America have a tendency to undergo successive splits, as one leader after another moves off with his following. In fact, some Evangelical movements seem to grow primarily in this manner, for an individual congregation is normally only as great as the leadership potential of the strongest person. A study of the membership of a number of local churches indicates that most of the members stand in some sort of dependency relationship to the "strong man" in the group. This certainly does not encourage other strong leaders to join such a church, for they instinctively shy away from being placed in such a dependency relationship.

Aesthetics

Even in the area of artistic forms, the conflict between authoritarianism and individualism is noticeable. The authoritarian tendency expresses itself in "dictated standards" and traditional models. In probably no art gallery in the world is one likely to see as many persons copying the old masters as in the Prado in Madrid, and some of this same desire to duplicate the past is present in many aesthetic forms of the New World.

Certainly in no part of the world is the word of a "royal academy" accepted with such implicit faith as in the case of the Royal Academy's *Dictionary of the Spanish Language*. Despite a highly productive and creative period of Spanish literature in the Siglo de Oro, much of the literature in Spanish during the colonial period was characterized by artificiality of themes and a baroque style. Until Rómulo Gallegos' novel *Doña Bárbara*, very few writers in Latin America realized they could write about the world in which they lived.

In the area of elocution or declamation one also discovers the heavy hand of an artificial tradition which makes of poetic recitations something rather "out of this world" — where special intonation, voice pitch, and pronunciation all combine to produce an unnatural and melodramatic effect.

Nevertheless, despite such traditionalism in many aspects of aesthetics, the Latin world is famous for its revolutionary artists and art. Few artists in the history of the world have matched the vigor and power of such muralists as Rivera, Orozco, and Siqueiros. In architecture Latins have often been far more radical than their North American colleagues — for example, the architectural monuments in Brazilia or the incredibly radical, but effective, buildings of the University of Mexico in Mexico City. The new museum of archaeology and anthropology in Mexico City is probably the most beautifully designed and has the most effectively displayed collection in the world.

The individualism of many folk artists in Latin America is manifested in their refusal to mass-produce their wares. Many of their designs are similar, but most artists refuse to be mere copyists.

In very large measure, both North America and Latin America have been largely dependent on Europe for their aesthetic models. But the average North American has been too busy to be much concerned about aesthetics, and many Latin Americans have been too much dominated by European developments to innovate. Where Mexican artists have distinguished themselves is in identifying with their Indian heritage. Out of the synthesis of European and indigenous art they have created vigorous and meaningful forms. By being willing to be themselves, rather than follow an authoritarian tradition, they have enriched the New World.

In the Evangelical churches in Latin America the area of aesthetics has largely been neglected. In the first place, many of the members of such churches have reacted so strongly against what they regarded as pictorial idolatry in the Roman Church that they have preferred the severe plainness of undecorated halls and chapels. Latin Evangelicals have often been encouraged in this by missionaries, who usually reflected the poorly developed tastes of lower-middle class North Americans. Nevertheless, Latin Evangelicals in the mission-sponsored churches have developed some of their own music and increasingly introduce pictures, although they are quite opposed to anything resembling sculpture.

On the other hand, in the indigenous Evangelical churches in Latin America which have not been the product (except quite indirectly) of missionary work, there are often interesting and effective uses of local musical forms and instruments, e.g. guitars, mandolins, and drums; and folk art, including beautifully embroidered altar cloths, polychromatic tile designs, the prominently displayed empty cross, and an abundant use of warm colors (pink, chartreuse, orange, and red) and in interior and exterior decoration. These are in radical contrast to the coldly white interiors of many mission-sponsored chapels.

Society

Historically the social structure of Latin America consisted primarily of two classes, the rich and the poor, with a very restricted class of intermediaries, the foreman or *mayordomo*. This situation, however, has radically changed. As of the present, Latin society can be best described as consisting of four classes.[14] The upper class is divided into two groups, the "old families," whose wealth consists largely in land (but who are increasingly investing in industry), and the "new families," who are the businessmen, industrialists, and top-ranking professionals, e.g. lawyers, doctors, etc. Actually, of course, many representatives of the "old families" belong to the professional classes, since in the universities they usually take some professional degree. But many of these persons remain largely dilettantes in their professions.

The growing middle class, which in many areas represents almost 20 percent of the urban population, consists of the "operators." These are the technicians, who will increasingly dominate the life of Latin America, for they have the specialized information necessary to make an industrial society operate.[15] Formerly these technicians were tied to the upper classes, which they attempted to emulate, but increasingly they are less inclined to do so, for they are developing a style of life of their own. As yet they are not class-conscious. Their position in the middle makes it difficult to be so, but their control of technical information makes them so necessary to the society that they need not feel insecure.

The lower classes consist primarily of two ranks, the factory workers and the farm laborers, with the former possessing considerably more prestige and receiving much greater economic rewards than the latter. As a result urbanization, with the corresponding alarming flight into the cities, is creating some of the most serious slum conditions found any place in the world.

The structure of society has been ideally viewed by many Latins as representing a pyramid, with the leadership conspicuously at the top and the masses of the poor at the bottom. All of this has been regarded traditionally as a kind of preordained structure, dependent upon birth. In fact, the old adage, *Nacer pobre es un delito* "It is a crime to be born poor," certainly stands in bold contrast to the North American equalitarian formula, "To be born poor is no disgrace."

Such a hierarchically structured society requires that each person recognize his position and his dependency relationships. This concept has been formulated neatly in the saying: *Un indio sin patrón es como rueda sin eje* "An Indian without a master is like a wheel without an axle." But if the peon requires a master, so does the master require peons; therefore mutual dependency—largely for the benefit of the upper classes—became the justification for the pyramidal structure of society.

This structure quite naturally had to be maintained not merely by appropriate political action to discourage those who might want to overthrow it but by social techniques which would reinforce the dependency relationships. These were accomplished primarily by marriage within the class (while, of course, permitting mistresses outside of one's class) and by the *compadrazgo* system (the god-father relationship).

As for threats which might come from foreigners who did not keep their place, such persons could be dealt with by social ostracism and economic reprisals, whether these were well-to-do gringos, who tended to be in conflict with the top of the social scale, or poor immigrants, who competed at the other extreme. Some groups often had to be restrained by force, the usual technique applied against the Indian uprisings in the Andean areas of South America.

Interestingly enough, in Latin America miscegenation did not prove to be the issue it became in North America. Since there was no real economic or social competition with so-called "inferior peoples," persons of Spanish background normally took the position that a mixture of "Latin blood" would only help the inferior persons and not endanger the position of the dominant population. Moreover, assimilation was relatively rapid, for anyone who possessed even a small amount of "Latin blood" was no longer regarded as an Indian or Negro but as a member of the dominant group. In contrast with this, in the United States anyone with any noticeable Indian or Negro traits was regarded as non-White. In other words, in Latin America even a small amount of white blood made a man *gente decente* (admitted him to Latin society), while in North America a similar amount of nonwhite blood excluded a person from White society.

To defend one's position within the Hispanoamerican social structure has generally been regarded as a man's prime duty. In fact, his personal honor has compelled him to react strongly to any threat to his position, which he more often than not has regarded as somewhat higher than it really was—a theme so effectively portrayed in the famous Mexican comic strip *La Familia Burron*. To symbolize and reinforce this social system, Latin Americans have developed an elaborate system of etiquette, often with ludicrous results. For example, in earlier times in the narrow streets of Mexico City a coach had to back out if a person of higher rank entered the street from the other end. On one occasion two men, each regarding himself as superior to the other, sat in such a street for an entire day, each waiting for the other to back out—only at last to reach a compromise of both backing out at the same time.

In view of the intense social controls imposed by the authoritarian structure of society, it is no wonder that Latins have had to find some emotional outlet in which the rigid restrictions on the individual could be at least temporarily swept away. The answer to this was found in the fiesta. In the same way that the revolution was the revolt of the individual against political authoritarianism, so the fiesta has constituted the revolt against social authoritarianism and control. In the fiesta social laws are broken, class distinctions are erased, drunkenness permits one to reveal himself (and thus escape from the constant pressures of self-defense), and intimate contact among people overcomes the usual social distance maintained by different classes.

In the fiesta the Latin is not so concerned with enjoying himself as with transcending himself.[16] From the festival, with its mixture of evil and holy (drunkenness and prayers, *aguardiente* and processions), the society emerges "purified," in the sense that the accumulated tensions are reduced and the group can return to the normalcy of hierarchically structured contacts.[17] It is significant to note that those societies which are the most desperate are also those which tend to engage in the most fiestas. Such social explosions are not required when opportunities exist for real, rather than symbolic, change. But even in the fiesta, with all its ecstasy, song, and shouting, the communication is largely a monologue, not a dialogue[18] —an exposure without response, a catharsis without replenishment.

Part of the intense desire for self-expression no doubt reflects the often mentioned "Latin pride," a kind of consuming desire to vindicate oneself in the face of any and all opposition, the type of pride which can shout, *Muera yo; viva mei fama* "Let me die; but let my fame live on."[19] This type of pride, which regards the society as merely the platform on which the charismatic individual acts out his commanding role, also expresses itself in many routine and mundane ways. The strong resistance of Mexican workers to suggestions for improving their work,[20] the tendency for students in schools to react strongly to criticism, and the impulsiveness with which a maid may walk out of a job if she thinks she has been unduly criticized, all point to a highly developed sense of personal pride, as perhaps a necessary and understandable reaction to the heavy authoritarian climate in which so many persons are forced to live and work.

Personal pride no doubt also reflects itself in other and even more subtle ways. The widespread Latin reaction against "opening oneself" (that is, revealing one's motivations and feelings)[21] is another manner in which people instinctively insist on masking their own feelings, as a matter of self-defense. Thus, somewhere within the inner soul of man is a precinct which the authoritarian world just cannot touch. By refusing to expose oneself, the self has still been preserved, in all its essential pride and honor. Even the widespread use of masks in fiestas may be symbolic of this desire not to expose one's true self.

Revolt against the social structure may take a number of

forms. The bandit gang which preys upon the rich, the *pandillas* (gangs of young boys) who refuse to fit into the social structure and are in revolt against it, and the political revolutionary in the universities are more often than not in actual revolt against the society as a whole rather than merely in conflict with the police or university authorities.

In North America also many people are in revolt against the establishment, but the revolt takes quite different forms. Conflict with the values of a hypocritical, affluent society leads many North Americans into beatnik and hippy revolt but not into fiestas, for North American society provides more social mobility. Most North Americans do not require fiestas to relieve the psychological tensions produced by an authoritarian social structure. For some minority groups, however, the riot becomes a sociological mechanism similar to the fiesta.

Another form of revolt in Hispanoamerican life is the strong reaction of many workers to the introduction of machines. On the level of the worker and especially on the level of the intellectual, machines are often regarded as enslaving man.[22] They are part of the inhuman physical world against which man must struggle. On the other hand, many North Americans look upon the machine as an instrument for relieving man of his physical toil, a means for providing him freedom and leisure. The machine is a labor-saving device, not a labor-robbing tool.

As a most helpful defense of personal pride, many Latins feel personal failure or guilt much less acutely than some people, especially those in the Protestant, Puritanical tradition. Since fate bears such a large share of blame for one's position in life and since sin is basically a matter of the weakness of the flesh (i.e. the fact of being a human being) rather than some perversion of the will, one can still defend one's personal integrity despite moral inadequacies.

The Evangelical Church in Latin America has experienced a number of serious difficulties as the result of the existing tensions between the authoritarian and individualistic views of society. In the first place, the Evangelical churches, which for the most part represent the lower-middle classes or upper-lower classes, have found it very difficult to appeal to persons in the upper classes. The

Protestant church quite understandably has a more complex problem than a corresponding Roman Catholic church would have, since the Protestant constituency forms a far more active congregation and participates much more in joint decisions, and since major policy decisions are made, at least theoretically, by the congregation as a whole and not by the hierarchy or clergy. This implies much more intimate interpersonal relationships than would be expected in a Roman Catholic church, where the congregation is not expected to form a social unit.

Evangelical churches also have problems due to their very rapid rise in the social structure. By virtue of quite new values, e.g. thrift, industry, and education of their children, Evangelicals experience a very rapid rise in economic position. This means that often they lose contact with the social environment out of which they have come— especially if the practices of such a group (e.g. fiestas) are regarded as not being acceptable to Protestant mores. The tendency for Evangelical groups to marry within their own constituencies also limits the range of their social contacts, and the fact that by becoming Evangelicals they are almost automatically removed from the *compadrazgo* system only accentuates their rupture with the social structure in which they live. With so many bridges to the former society destroyed, it is little wonder that they often find themselves quite restricted in social contacts. Having left their former associates, they find that they cannot readily establish new links with persons of their same economic standing in the Roman Catholic society.

The position of the North American missionary in this situation is especially difficult, for he has a very ambivalent role. On the one hand, he feels committed to working toward a completely independent church, especially one which is financially independent of foreign funds. But he still wants to guarantee that this church will stay within the fold of the mission-affiliated denomination. Having established such a church by the *patrón* system, in which he is the *patrón*, it is difficult to find leadership truly able to lead, for during the years he has tended to surround himself with followers, not with leaders. As a result many of the mission-sponsored churches have relatively weak Latin leaders. In contrast with this, the completely indigenous Protestant churches in

Latin America often have strong leaders, for they are the direct result of activity by persons who have come to the top because of their unusual charismatic qualities and their capacity to command.

The family

Within the Latin American family the tensions of authoritarianism and individualism are especially acute. The father's role is that of the *caudillo*-the *paterfamilias*—in every sense. He is expected not only to demand obedience but in some senses even to lord it over his children. The expression *Yo soy tu padre*, literally "I am your father," actually means "I am better than you are," hardly the ideal for so-called family sharing. Nevertheless, this position of the father does provide the Latin family with an authority structure and gives the son a much more solid authority figure than exists in many North American households.

The father of the family also demands obedience and faithfulness from his wife, who, though serving as an influential go-between in relationships between father and children, is nevertheless in a dependent relationship to the husband, both legally and socially.

The revolt of individualism in the family is strikingly displayed in the intergeneration tensions in Latin America. The political activism of university students against the government (an almost perennial problem, irrespective of the government in power) is interpreted by many as clear evidence of the revolt of young people against symbols of parental domination.

Since, however, the tensions of authoritarianism and individualism parallel so closely many aspects of *machismo* and *hembrismo*, it seems better to delay further consideration of certain of these generation problems until they can be considered in the broader light of the psychological problems arising out of tensions between the sexes.

Within the family structure one can see considerable differences between the patterns in Latin America and North America. Latins, for example, find it most difficult to understand how American fathers can be so relatively "weak" and so often dominated by their wives. It would be unthinkable for a Latin man to have to phone his wife to see if it were all right to bring a guest home for supper, but woe to the average North American who does not obtain clearance from his wife! This shift in roles in the North American context so puzzled one Latin that he asked this writer, "Why are all the men missionaries like women, and the women missionaries like men?" From the standpoint of many Latins, North America produces a very high percentage of weak-minded men and strong-minded women.

Within the Evangelical constituency in Latin America, church conflicts often result in splits along generational lines. The challenge to existing leadership comes as a rule from younger leadership—not necessarily from people in their teens, but from those who are regarded in a different generation as far as patterns of respect and authority are concerned.

But as important as the tension between authoritarianism and individualism may be, it only explains some of the strangely diverse patterns of behavior characteristic of Latin life. In order to see the picture in better perspective, we must add certain other dimensions, including the conflict between idealism and realism.

3
Idealism and Realism

The conflict between idealism and realism, so aptly and meaningfully symbolized in the joint figures of Don Quijote and Sancho Panza, has been recognized by many persons. They have seen in Cervantes' portrayal of the idealistic warrior, Don Quijote, and his realistic, earthy companion, Sancho Panza, the two dominant elements in the Latin character. Abelardo Villegas[1] equates *quijotismo* with Jacobinism and *sanchismo* with positivism. Other authors have seen parallel types of distinctions, but no one has dealt more effectively with this aspect of Latin personality and thought than Miguel de Unamuno,[2] who has repeatedly emphasized the disjuncture between the ideal and the real in Latin life and thought. At the same time one must beware of too simplistic an analysis, for it would be a serious mistake not to recognize the mixed motivations and even seemingly contradictory elements in both of Cervantes' famous symbolic characters.

In many ways idealism is an aspect of Latin American intellectualism, a search for transcendental values — *lo algo más allá*. This "spiritual" goal of life is evidenced in much of Latin literary activity, in the widespread use of poetic forms, and in areas of philosophical interest. Even a brief glance at the types of books placed in the show windows of bookstores in Latin America will convince anyone that the concern of many Latins is far more oriented toward the ideal than is the case with most North Americans.

On the other hand, Latins are also intensely concerned with the here and now. Despite soaring flights into the realm of the spirit, Latins do not escape from the body— in all its passion, sensuality, and earthiness. Though the poet's head may be in the clouds, his feet are usually well mired in the clay of sensual feelings.

Some persons have seen the tensions between idealism and realism worked out in historical developments.[3] For example, in the history of Mexico, it is claimed that before independence *sanchismo* (realism) was the dominant theme, but with independence *quijotismo* (idealism) became a dominant aspect of Mexican life. Under the domination of ecclesiastical institutions, however, *sanchismo* reasserted itself, and only in the Reform of the 1860s did *quijotismo* reassert itself. Once again, under Porfirio Diaz (with the emphasis on positivism) *sanchismo* ruled the day, only to be routed in the Revolution of 1910-17, when *quijotismo* took over. Such an analysis has many interesting features, but it is in many respects entirely too simplistic. Under the rule of Díaz, when positivism was the dominant philosophy and the reason (as well as the excuse) for keeping the peons under strict control, there was a great emphasis on the "ideal state" and the "ideological basis" of society.

Rather than experiencing first one and then the other aspect of the dichotomy of idealism and realism, Latin America has much more commonly had a blend of the two, for Don Quijote and Sancho Panza were constant companions rather than competitors. Octavio Paz[4] sees these tensions as producing the *mentiras* "lies" under which Latins have lived through the years: gaining independence, only to take on new masters; establishing republics, only to find themselves ruled by dictators; fighting for freedom, only to be enslaved by new forces or old powers in some new guise; and winning revolutions, only to discover that new despots have been thrust into power.[5]

Religion

In the realm of religion the theme of idealism (in its technical, philosophical sense) expresses itself theologically in providing all the answers while asking no questions. This is possible because dogma is "in the heavenlies," untouchable by human discourse or even by reason. Once it has been formulated, it must only be believed and defended, not examined. Such an "idealistic" approach to theology tends, of course, to separate theology from life and doctrines from experience.

Such a theological separation is made easier by an idealistic concept of man, for certainly in popular Roman Catholic theology sin is merely something associated with the body, since matter is basically sinful due to its essential weakness. Thus sin is an aspect of having a body, and the popular excuse for sinning is *Yo soy carne,* literally "I am flesh," but equivalent to "I am only human." If under such circumstances the will can remain pure, even though the body may be sinful, then the prostitute can have an image of Santa María Magdalena on her dresser and the thief can take some of the proceeds from stolen goods and buy a candle to burn before his patron saint.

Such separation between the body and the will and between theology and life is made even easier by the tendency toward rather radical separation into categories of the sacred and the secular. If, as most persons believe, the first can sanctify the latter, then all that is required is an omnipotent God and an eternal Church in order to make all of life ultimately acceptable.

This distinction between the sacred and the secular is symbolized quite effectively in the role of the priest who gives himself entirely to the sacred, without concerns for family and secular interests. Moreover, the priest's functions are not dependent on his own holiness but on his consecration to his task. He may sanctify the elements without himself being holy, and he may declare a person innocent without being guiltless himself. Such institutional-ized distinctions between the secular and the sacred inevitably result in the separation of the priest from the people, and the higher the priest is elevated the lower may the people live, for they are vicariously identified with the priest, even though their lives reflect little of the holiness which is supposed to characterize his life.

The idealistic approach to life is also effectively demonstrated in laws preventing divorce. The indissolubility

of marriage is, of course, the theological ideal, but recognition of the fact that all human beings cannot attain to
the ideal means that one is forced to accept some widespread
form of extramarital sexual attachment. Thus the Church
finds itself required to excommunicate those who divorce
while not rejecting those who keep mistresses. To force
one person out of the Church for getting a divorce but to
allow another to remain in it, even though he supports one
or more mistresses, places the Church in a completely
untenable position, from the standpoint of the North American
Protestant. However, this is not necessarily so for the
Latin. Divorce is a failure to keep one's house in order,
whereas having mistresses is an expression of the positive
value of *machismo*.

By being so thoroughly idealistic the Church has not,
however, escaped from this world or from the realistic
demands of life upon it. By asking no questions, religion
also expects no answers, and this means no involvement from
the layman. Why should he bother his head about religious
issues? Traditionally one was better off not to read the
Bible, for reading it might involve one in serious theological
difficulties. Therefore, theological illiteracy was considered
preferable to theological danger.

The disjuncture between the spiritual ideal and the earthly
real is in some measure resolved by the confessional, but
this often results in a relatively low day-by-day standard of
behavior, for the flesh can be thoroughly bad as long as the
spirit is thoroughly cleansed. Traditionally, compromises
between the ideal and the real were sold in the form of
indulgences, and even today some of these practices remain.
Among Latins in the southwestern United States it has been
normal to receive indulgence to eat meat during Lent for
the payment of $5.00, and soldiers have been offered mem-
bership in the Society for the Propagation of the Faith for
the payment of a fitting sum of money.

Obviously the Church has never been able to escape the
demands of the temporal world. Sometimes this took place
in concessions to paganism, so that in many areas a kind of
Christo-paganism arose. In other circumstances the conflict
between the ideal and real took the radical form of the
auto-da-fé, in which the body was destroyed in order to
preserve the spirit (based on 1 Corinthians 5.5). This made

it possible to deal with captured enemies in the New World in an ideal as well as a practical way. Such persons could be baptized, with all the touching formalities required, and then they could be impaled on sharp stakes and shot through with arrows.

One reaction to the ideal of the spirit is no doubt the preoccupation with the death of the body—the cult of death and the contemplation of horror. The Latin world is also the realm of the bloody Christ, the area where the skull and crossbones are not merely a symbol of poison and where the writing of mock epitaphs is a kind of macabre humor. In Mexico the bullfight has been described as the bloody mass of the masses—where death can be stared in the face, at least vicariously. Such concern for death has also meant that Good Friday, not resurrection morning, is the high point of Easter; for on Good Friday the crowds vie with one another "to bury God" (perhaps they secretly desire to bury themselves), but on Sunday morning relatively few people are present to celebrate Christ's rising from the dead.

This focus on the realism of death finds another outlet in spiritism, with its communication with the souls of the dead and the sense of group belonging and participation in death. Strangely enough, most spiritists feel no special contradiction between what they engage in and the teachings of the Church.

Reactions of North Americans to the forms of Roman Catholicism in Latin America have been especially strong among the Maryknoll Fathers, whose detailed studies of Latin Christendom and the serious departures from biblical faith have been both thorough and critical—far more so than anything which has been written by Protestants. North American Roman Catholic laymen are often quite shocked by what they see in Latin America—they cannot believe their eyes. A church-sponsored fiesta in an Indian town in South America is often so radically different from worship in a Roman Catholic church in the United States as to make one wonder how the two could even be remotely related.

It would be wrong to think, however, that the Evangelical Church in Latin America has totally escaped the problems posed by the tensions between the ideal and the real demands on life and thought. Protestants often insist on correct doctrine regardless of behavior. This means that emphasis is often placed on the verbal formulas rather than on the resultant life. The churches become well known for their declarations of faith—more so than for their demonstrations of a new life.

During revivals great attention is focused on verbal confession—not to a priest but to the congregation or to God, yet often the repentant person soon slips back into the old way of life. In fact, most people in the congregation more or less expect he will do just that—and it is rare that he does not live up to this expectation.

This struggle to reconcile the ideal and the real also makes the average Latin American much more intense in worship than his North American counterpart. The conflict is real, and there is no time for frivolity and triviality in worship.[6] A missionary's pulpit humor is rarely appreciated, for in the context of life in which the great existential questions have not been resolved (they still stare people squarely in the face) there is no time for idle words.

In certain regards many Evangelicals in Latin America have a rather bleak emotional existence. They find sustenance in their faith but little support in their interpersonal relationships and very limited room for emotional expression in a group. In many mission-sponsored churches the new converts often grow emotionally cold and even indifferent. In contrast, the indigenous churches place great emphasis on emotionally stimulating experiences. In fact, in some churches almost every service is a fiesta in miniature. The people become "drunk with the Spirit," rather than with wine, and no doubt for some persons this type of release from the daily grind of their emotionally impoverished lives provides the stimulus for at least a possible and even a meaningful existence.

Philosophy

The idealistic implications in philosophical inquiry have always been a dominant theme in Hispanoamerican life, for people are fascinated by the theoretical aspects of doctrines and precepts. But as Unamuno has said so clearly, for the Latin "doctrine is the theory of proper conduct, not a guide to it."[7]

There has been through the years a deep concern for

philosophy, and especially for the philosophy of the spirit. This has meant repeated repudiation of materialism as a philosophy, and nowhere has this been more effectively enunciated than in José Enrique Rodó's essay on *Ariel and Calibán*, in which he likens Ariel to the Latin American who reaches for the sky, and Calibán to the North American who grovels in the ground of materialism.

Popular philosophy in Latin America also shows great concern for the ideal, the theoretical, and the "spiritual." Interest in theosophy, universalism, and Rosicrucianism reflects this thrust into the realm of the spirit.

Popular philosophy also takes certain practical forms— with idealistic dimensions: the redemption of life by revolution, the passion for the ideal life (worked out in Utopian schemes), and, as panaceas for Latin woes, the wholesale importation of philosophies from abroad (for example, positivism, existentialism, and Communism). But this has often produced even further tensions, for though the people's spirits were in Europe, their bodies were in America.[8] A basic insecurity, resulting from looking to Europe for models while actually borrowing more from North America,[9] only heightened the tension in many respects. One notes, for example, that when Latins go to the United States they often engage in a kind of ritual denunciation of North America, both immediately before and after such an experience. In fact, the intensity of the denunciation is often directly proportionate to the extent to which the person in question has assimilated North American concepts and values.

But though the Latin American strives for the spirit, "his deepest self aspires to be flesh, and to live a full, concrete, fleshly existence."[10] He is not only a Don Quijote charging philosophical windmills, but equally a hungry Sancho Panza whose principal concern is getting plenty to eat. Yet even in the area of philosophy the focus is not on the rational but on the intuitional, not on mind but on feeling. Abelardo Villegas insists that philosophy in Mexico is essentially emotive rather than reasoned;[11] he contends that this intuition is basically "irrational," [12] and as such coincides with the Latin propensity to avoid anything which means work or discipline. His criticism may be rather too severe, but it comes from a Latin, not from a North American.

Nevertheless, even in the midst of formulating Utopian schemes, Latins remain realistically pessimistic. This theme is frequently reflected in poetry and song:

No vale nada la vida	Life is worthless
La vida no vale nada	Worthless is life
Comienza siempre llorando	It always begins with crying
Y así llorando se acaba	It always end with tears
Por eso es que en este mundo	And so it is in this world
La vida no vale nada.[13]	Life is worthless.

This type of earthy pessimism, based on decades of suffering, helps to explain not only the cheapness of human life in the Latin world but also the incredible courage that many Latins have in the face of death. As Samuel Ramos has insisted, Mexicans have in the past only "known how to die,"[14] but what is now required is the wisdom to know how to live.

Such basic pessimism does not expect revolutions to succeed in their goals or candidates to fulfill their promises. Hence all men are free to get what they can as long as there is anything more to get.

As a confirmed pragmatist (at least in practice if not in theory), the North American has little time for and even less understanding of the Latin American's concern for the philosophical ideal. For the North American it is not a matter of "What is its ultimate meaning?" but "What is its present-day value?" Moreover, such values are usually symbolized in things. In fact, in discussions with Latins a North American more likely than not will insist on the superiority of North American culture because in the United States more people have telephones, radios, two cars, television sets, bathtubs, and flush toilets. For Latins such reasoning is only sure proof that Rodó was right in his descriptions of Ariel and Calibán.

In addition to being a pragmatist at heart, the average North American is also an eclectic in his thinking. He is not worried if his ideas stem from quite different philosophical systems or even if they are contradictory. Usually in any discussion of philosophy with an educated Latin, the North American is quite lost, for he thinks that people study or read philosophy only if they are either impractical or somewhat queer. He is not concerned to "know reality," only to make use of it. In this sense, the North American is a realist, but an optimistic, not a pessimistic, one.

These radical differences in Latin American and North American ways of thinking appear to stem from quite different concepts of the world—described by anthropologists as "concepts of limited and unlimited good." In general the North American believes in unlimited good. That is to say, "the sky is the limit," and there are always rewards for anyone who will strive long enough and hard enough to get them. Moreover, no one need think that in procuring benefits for himself, he is necessarily depriving others of what is their due, for the world contains plenty for everyone.

In contrast with this optimistic appraisal of unlimited opportunities and rewards, most Latin Americans look upon the world as consisting of limited good. The success of one man almost inevitably involves the failure of another, for in the rigid hierarchy of both people and things changes mean mutual displacements. One rises only as others fall. Moreover, the treasure of the world (symbolically, the gold of the Western Hemisphere) is limited, and it is only for the first to get there and for the brave who endure. But fate more than effort and luck more than work determine success.

The North American concept of the unlimited good took root in a land with seemingly limitless frontiers, uncalculable riches in land and minerals, and incredibly rapid growth of industry and technology. In Latin America, on the contrary, even what land there was (though quite unexploited) was nevertheless ceded to large landowners. Mineral wealth belonged technically to the State—as the inheritor of the crown—and wealth remained locked firmly in the control of a limited number of ruling families who constituted the oligarchy of most Hispanoamerican lands. It is scarcely any wonder, therefore, that so many Latins developed a pessimistic view of progress and tended to find philosophical escape or justification in nonmaterial values.

At the same time, Latin Americans increasingly have sought self-fulfillment in feelings and emotions, not in possessions but in being. The Latin American scholar might not marshal many facts to support his case, but he has certainly not been short in perception of human values or in brilliant insights into human motivations. While the North American treatises seem coldly calculating and overburdened with statistical tables and mathematical formulas, Latin essays have been warmly human, filled with emotion and sesitive to the "higher values."

Within the Evangelical Church in Latin America the tendency to idealism has often taken the form of heavy "doctrinal preaching," in which ideal behavior has been proclaimed and the opposite condemned. Such preaching has usually started with a text and often has not departed far enough from it to touch living situations. The Utopian ideal has been clearly proclaimed, and most of the listeners sigh a kind of vicarious assent while condemned to continue in their other world of the flesh. In their realism they are generally quite pessimistic about their chances of ever entering by the "narrow gate."

Too often this pessimism, mixed with cynicism, tends to undercut plans for reform and revival, even before programs have been begun. This does not mean that people withhold their verbal agreement—in fact, they often shout their approval almost directly in proportion to their pessimism as to the chances of success. Perhaps this is in the hope that verbal support may act as a kind of imitative magic, so that in some way or other success may be attained.

This means that Evangelical churches place a great premium on verbalization, but not necessarily of the reasoned and informative variety. Actually, people want much more to feel than to think, and hence the really popular preacher is one who appeals to the emotions, not to the mind. Too often the mission-sponsored church has a service which resembles a classroom in which one studies facts rather than talks to God. On the contrary, the indigenous Pentecostal groups have appealed strongly to the feelings, for even though one may not be able to understand fully the message, one cannot help but feel the impact of group worship and the dynamic of the emotional outbursts.

Politics

In the political realm idealism has meant the promulgation of "perfectionist laws." The systems of social security in some countries in Latin America are absolute models, but the administration is sometimes so hopelessly inadequate that much of the good in the laws is lost. The slogan *leyes perfectas y costumbres podridas* "perfect laws and rotten practices" is a telling indictment of the tendency to make laws perfect while expecting that practice will be something quite different. In some instances laws have been hopelessly impossible. According to one traffic law in the state of Veracruz, Mexico, a driver of a bus was supposed to stop some fifty yards from a railroad crossing and carefully look in both directions. He was then to advance within about two yards of the tracks and again stop, get out of the bus, and look in both directions. Only then was he to proceed over the tracks, but at such a velocity that his bus would not stop on the tracks, even if the motor stalled. Quite obviously, under such conditions there would be no possibility of an accident, but equally obviously, no bus driver was going to obey the law. Hence, the law did not prevent accidents, but only insured that the bus driver would be found guilty if an accident occurred.

Even when revolutions have been won, the Utopian solutions promoted by the victors are frequently so unrealistic as to defeat the very purpose of the struggle. *Hágase la justicia aunque perezca el mundo* "Let justice be done, even though the world is destroyed in the process" [15] is too frequently applicable to many of the well-intentioned but poorly conceived approaches to remaking the world. Samuel Ramos[16] insists that this basic failure to adjust the ideal solution to the realities of the situation has left a most damaging mark upon the average Mexican's unconsciously internalized system of values.

In government the majority party often attempts to act as though there were simply no minority—no opposition. A wonderful ideal for any politician, but a tragic failure for the society. Ideally, any party in power wants to eliminate graft and bribery. Hence responsibility is divided and every official document requires a host of signatures. In reality, however, this only means dividing the spoil, not eliminating the bribe. Moreover, divided responsibility means that no one can be held accountable.

One should not, however, think that Latins are naively idealistic about politics. Quite the contrary. They are undoubtedly some of the most realistic and insightful persons in the world when it comes to evaluating political motives and working out acceptable compromises. The law is, of course, ideal—as untouchable as dogma—but the interpretation of the law is another matter, and here is where the human element enters in. Law, in fact, is consistently "transcended" by friendship, for as one says in Latin America, "The law is only for those whom one does not know; all the benefits of the law are for one's friends, and all the rigors of the law are for one's enemies." The goddess of justice in Latin America is not blind, for if she were, there would be no way to administer law with due regard to human differences. Naturally, transcending the law is principally the prerogative of the strong person.

Sometimes a perverse blend of idealism and realism results in a vicious circle in government. For example, many petty officials in government receive such low salaries that they almost have to supplement their income by what are not called bribes but "fees for services." Higher government officials know this, but they do not see any point in raising salaries, for that would seemingly not stop the practice of the "fees." On the other hand, to stop the practice of fees without raising salaries would mean that many government officials simply could not support their families.

If, however, one wants to be protected against large grafters in government, it seems to many Latins that one is better advised not to put a poor man in office, but rather a rich one—even one who is suspected of having become rich from graft—for now that he is rich he is not under such constraint to accept bribes as is the poor man, who would not be able to exist on a government salary.

Even though the party in power would ideally like to govern as though the minority did not exist, in reality a high percentage of governments in Latin America make quite good provision for certain leaders of the opposition, even to the point of being accused at times of buying the support of the opposition. If Latins are anything, they are realists.

Part of the difference between the ideal and real political structure can be explained by the division of responsibility which exists in so many instances of local, and sometimes of national, government. In such cases the politicians are often only the *mayordomos* "foremen"

who take orders from the *dueños* "owners." The really
influential persons do not run for office, and they are well
known only to the small oligarchy of which they are a part.
But they have the power. They do not, however, have to
take political responsibility for their decisions, since
they can change candidates almost as easily as a coach
can substitute players in a game. Nevertheless, by
dividing political power, one can preserve a greater facade of
idealism, while at the same time being more realistic
about practical circumstances.

The North American has the tendency to criticize the
Latin American for political hypocrisy and dishonesty—
rarely realizing, or at least admitting, how far the political
structure of his own country has departed from its presumed
ideals and how relatively ludicrous such events as presidential conventions appear to people in other parts of the world.
The Latin American, on the other hand, is much more a
"political animal" than the North American, and he sees
through much of the political hokum in North America.
Moreover, he also feels that the North American is too
much bound to laws—too rigid in his view of violations
and too unsympathetic to the demands of friendship. The
North American, on the other hand, feels that the Latin is
guilty of favoritism. The Latin concludes that the North
American is too mechanistic in his views of justice and
hence basically immoral.

This problem of idealism and realism in law and government shows up in certain aspects of the Evangelical
movement in Latin America. Missionaries, for example,
are often shocked to see how very little the church constitutions mean when people become involved in some congregational dispute. Having helped to write such constitutions
and having even taught the people how to follow Robert's
Rules of Order, the missionary is naive enough to think
that political problems within the church can be readily
resolved by congregational meetings in which issues
can be openly stated and decisions made with fairness to
all concerned. But in Latin America real decisions are
not made by such formal structures—any more than they
are in North America. Rather, a small group (usually
smaller than in a corresponding North American context)
actually makes the decisions, and if one knows in advance

who is related to whom or who speaks to whom about what
(the communication network of the congregation, reflecting
the real, not the ideal, authority structure), the results
of any vote can largely be predicted.

Aesthetics

In the aesthetic realm the tensions between the ideal and
the real produce some of the most interesting and creative
forms. In speech and literature these conflicts have sometimes resulted in the highest stylistic forms being employed
to discuss the most sordid situations, for the strong
idealistic urge has tended to delay the kind of literary
revolution which has occurred in the novel and in poetry
in many other parts of the Western world.

In folk music there is also evidence of the blend between
the ideal and the real—reaching for the stars while being
earthily cynical. A song with the theme of *canta dolores*
"singing of woes" combines an exhilarating music with
pessimistic words—typical of much folk music in Latin
America.

Aesthetics might be regarded as a kind of substitute
religion for many persons in Latin America, since it is
in aesthetic expression that persons can make the sacrifice
of earthly forms and substances to the spirit of eternal
design and form. Abelardo Villegas divided the arts into
three types: Apollonian, Dyonisiac, and mystic, in which
the Apollonian represents reason, the Dyonisiac the emotions
and passions, and the mystic the transcendence of the eternal
in what is still fully human.[17] In this very analysis one can
readily detect the constant tension between the ideal and
the real.

In practical life Latins also exhibit this blend: the tender
care for flowers by those living in the most sordid slums;
the decoration of walls with brightly colored pictures,
artificial flowers, embroidery, and designs in some of the
poorest homes; the widespread production of folk art in the
decoration of ordinary objects—oxcart wheels in Costa Rica,
everyday household pottery in Mexico, and shawls in many
parts of Latin America.

Many North Americans find it hard to appreciate the
passion and emotion in Latin music and art. The decorations

in the fiestas are thought to be too bright and the colors of some buildings (for example, pink or chartreuse) are considered shocking. On the other hand, the Latin American finds it difficult to understand North American home architecture. The idea of having a home "blend with nature" is clearly meaningless, for it is contrast with nature—the struggle against nature—which is distinctive for man.

Within the Evangelical Church in Latin America aesthetic developments have scarcely had a chance to express themselves, for the standards have too often been dictated by those whose tastes have been quite alien to Latin forms. Though music has been encouraged, it has usually been merely an adaptation of hymns used in North America, and only the most typical 19th-century religious illustrations have been encouraged. In the indigenous Protestant churches much of this has been changed. Considerable use has been made of Latin music and instruments. Ranchero bands and orchestras are not uncommon in such churches, and the quality of their music is in many cases excellent. In one church in Ixmiquilpan, Mexico, there are four groups of musicians who make full use of typical Mexican instruments, guitars, mandolins, guitarrons, and tuned jars. A high percentage of the music represents an indigenous hymnody, in which biblical themes, as applied to living situations, are sung to the glory of God and the admonition of the believers. This church also has a striking painting of "the waters of baptism." Rather than some dull reproduction of a typical scene from the bank of the River Jordan, this picture contains a massive snow-clad mountain from the base of which flows a tremendous torrent of water. This is symbolic of the purifying effects of baptism, but even more it represents the meaning of life-giving water in this semi-desert region of Central Mexico.

Society

For the upper class one traditional ideal has been avoidance of manual labor. Unamuno calls it *nuestro castizo horror al trabajo* "our horror of work," and he cites the saying: "Nothing lowers a man so much as having to earn a living as a common laborer." Physical work is interpreted as denying one's capacity for "spiritual" activity and rewards coming from such enterprises. In this sense the upper class has identified its role with the "sacred" functions, which sanctify the rest of life by giving it meaning and control.

In interpersonal contacts Latin society has also sought to preserve the ideal more than the real through the practice of telling people what they want to learn rather than disturbing them with the blunt truth. This is not really lying, but simply placing higher values on ideal interpersonal relationships than on truth. It must be remembered that all societies have their standard forms of misrepresentation, and in North American life these are especially prominent in the introductions of VIP's, in eulogies at funerals, in letters of resignation, and in acceptance of such letters.

In certain customs Latins also preserve the forms of both the ideal and the real. Even today many Latin homes have very strict rules covering courtship and chaperons, but chaperons are often conveniently deaf and sometimes seemingly blind. Virginity of the bride is still the ideal, although her real condition seems little hindrance to marriage, and few people seem overly concerned—unless someone is foolish enough to make a fuss (that is, to spoil the game), and then "all hell breaks loose," for honor must be defended.

Ideally and theoretically, the *compadrazgo* system is an excellent device for insuring that no child will be in want, for it is a technique by which those above assume responsibility for those beneath. In reality, however, the *compadrazgo* system is often a technique for social climbing. There is almost always a *quid pro quo* and an exchange relationship is set up. The godfather not only assumes some responsibility for the education of the new child, but he counts on the support of the parents of the child in any economic or social crisis. They become, in a sense, his retainers, and they must exhibit the expected loyalty, or the godfather feels little or no compulsion to comply with his vowed obligation.

For the North American, perhaps the most difficult thing to understand about a Latin American is the traditional attitude toward physical work. The North American has imbibed so much of the Puritan ethic that he is convinced that work is a kind of therapeutic in itself. He even exercises in order to be able to work longer, and many persons take a vacation in order to be able to work better the next year. All of this seems pathetically stupid to Latin Americans, who have traditionally regarded work as a means of enjoying nonwork.

These attitudes toward work are, however, based on other more fundamental considerations. The North American is much more concerned with the physical reality of life— matter over which he claims mastery and which he is determined to harness to his benefit and ideally to that of all mankind. In contrast with this attitude, the Latin American often regards physical reality as something so impersonal as to be largely controlled by fate. Therefore, he is much more inclined to put a higher premium on interpersonal values and relationships. These he feels he can change, for they are part of the richly human world of which he is a part. Most Latin Americans are actually much better in dealing with interpersonal problems than are North Americans,[18] for this is their world. It is not strange, therefore, that so many Latin Americans regard North Americans as crude, tactless, and insensitive in their interpersonal relationships. In any event, the average Latin American is much better able to "see through" a North American than the reverse, and this is especially true when the North American thinks he is being cleverly diplomatic. If he really wants to deceive, he should be "stupidly frank," for this is certainly not what his Latin counterpart would ever be.

Within the Evangelical Church in Latin America, these real and ideal issues in the social structure have had serious consequences. The missionary generally fills the role of the *patrón* or the *dueño*, for he supplies the funds. The pastor is the *mayordomo* who acts as the go-between, but in view of his social identification with the upper class (since he is the special representative of the *dueño*), he is a professional and as such is not supposed to engage in work with his hands. Thus to raise a garden or to supplement his income with a trade has seemed beneath his dignity, especially if he has gone off to a seminary or Bible school and has earned a "degree." On the other hand, sheer economic necessity often forces a change in this traditionally prevailing pattern.

At the same time, in this type of situation it is very difficult to encourage a ministry of the laity. Religious functions are supposed to be carried out by professionals, who are specifically paid to perform this work. Why should one person do another's work? Moreover, the pastor is often reluctant to encourage too much responsibility on the part of the layman, for this would seem to diminish the strategic importance of his role as the *mayordomo*.

The family

Within the family ideally there is no divorce, but in reality there is often severe estrangement, involving keeping mistresses and going to prostitutes.

Similarly, in the ideal household the father is the head, but in reality the mother, as will be seen even more clearly in the next chapter, is the real emotional center of the family. As the ideal head of the household, the father does have the authority, although often he does not carry the responsibility for the support of the family. Thus in many poor households there may be a succession of men, and only the mother remains the integrating force.

So acute becomes the difference between the real and the ideal roles in the family structure that many wives simply do not expect love and marriage to be synonymous — a fact cynically expressed in the saying: *Que mi marido me dé a mí los pesos, y a otra los besos* "Let my husband give the money to me, and the kisses to someone else."[19] This marital relationship may become so distorted by the ideal-real conflict that one can actually find a prayer such as Dr. María Elvira Bermúdez cites: *Dios mío, que mi marido no me engañe, y si me engaña, que yo no lo sepa; y si lo sé, que no me importe* "My God, may my husband not deceive me, but if he does deceive me, then may I not know about it; however, if I do learn about it, then may it make no difference to me."[20] One can scarcely think of a North American woman uttering such a petition.

In North America there is probably no less marital infidelity. It simply takes different forms. There is not much of a tendency for mistresses, but monogamy is extremely brittle. In Latin America the patterns are rapidly changing, for with increased education, more equality before the law, and economic independence (an increasing number of middle class and even upper class women work), the ideal role of the submissive wife is rapidly becoming anachronistic in certain sectors of society.

Latin Americans, however, find it quite difficult to understand North American family life. The failure of the North American father to fulfill his ideal role as head of the house seems incomprehensible, and the unruliness of many American children becomes added confirmation of the chaotic structure of North American life.

Within the Evangelical Church, the real issue with respect to family life centers on divorce, remarriage, and common law relationships. In many instances persons have become separated from their legal spouses and have struck up common law relationships, often remaining faithful to one another for many years, rearing a family, and providing well for them. Finally, these persons may become interested in the gospel as preached in some Evangelical church. If, however, this church is mission-sponsored, such persons soon discover that they cannot be admitted as members or receive communion until they are married. In some countries, however, it is impossible for them to get a divorce. In other situations they have lost all contact with their former spouse and hence cannot arrange for a divorce. What are such persons to do? In general, they will be told that if they believe in Jesus Christ and live good lives, they will of course go to heaven, but they cannot be admitted into the membership of the church unless they are legally married. Nevertheless, they cannot become legally married. This means that actually the membership of the church has become more exclusive than the membership of heaven—an interesting anomaly, to say the least. Many indigenous Evangelical churches, however, take quite a different view of such developments. They quite naturally do all they can to arrange for a couple to be legally married, but when there are laws or circumstances preventing this, such persons are not excluded from membership or full participation. As one Evangelical leader explained it, "We all are caught up in the injustices of this world, and we must not exclude anyone for whom Christ died and whom he has accepted." It is little wonder that this type of approach has had a wide appeal to many of the socially dispossessed in Latin America, who crave acceptance and need love from those who are willing to let grace supersede law.

4
Machismo and Hembrismo

The masculine-feminine opposition occurs in all cultures, but in Latin culture this contrast has assumed unusually heightened and dramatic dimensions,[1] while in Mexico it is probably more accentuated than in other areas of Latin America. As Abelardo Villegas[2] has said, the average Mexican may regard the European as having more culture, the North American as having more money, but the Mexican as being more masculine (*muy macho*). This Don Juan complex expresses itself in many ways: in the quality of a man's mistresses, in the number of women whom he has "conquered," and in the undisputed supremacy of the father within the family—involving also at least an outward form of self-sacrifice and subjection on the part of the mother.

Strong emphasis on *machismo* inevitably produces the complementary *hembrismo* , or extreme female passivity and dependence. At the same time *machismo* , though catering to male dominance, also implies considerable dependence on females, who must constitute the "stage" upon which the male acts out his dominant role. Being constantly motivated to exhibit his dominance also produces a measure of insecurity in the male—an aspect of the two-edged sword of values which will become more evident as we examine further implications of the *machismo - hembrismo* tension.

If, however, we are to understand the precise manner in which the *machismo-hembrismo* contrast affects Latin life, it will be necessary to analyze its implications in the whole realm of behavior, beginning with the family.

The family

Any analysis of *machismo-hembrismo* must begin with a study of the family, for it is here that the tensions are the most severe, and it is in the context of the family that this contrast develops many implications for the rest of Latin life.

The Latin ideal of masculine valor was, of course, a dominant theme throughout medieval life, but perhaps in no part of Western Europe was it more emphasized than in Spain, where valor became closely identified with being strongly masculine in sexual capacity and general behavior.

In the New World, the ideal of being *muy macho* expressed itself quite naturally in the dominance of the *conquistadores* over native women, for the conquerors of the new lands did not come with their families but with the purpose of exploiting and then returning to Europe. The children born of such temporary unions of conquerors and Indian women often felt strongly resentful of the "absent, irresponsible father." At the same time, *mestizo* boys no doubt desired to be every bit as *macho* as the father had been.

As Santiago Ramírez[3] and others have analyzed this situation, it would appear that the *mestizo* boy was emotionally attached to his mother, who provided the only real security he had. But this Indian mother belonged to a socially inferior and despised class. To attain status in a world dominated by a conquering race, a *mestizo* male had to exhibit the same *macho* characteristics that were so closely identified with the father. This immediately set up conflicting loyalties. Being emotionally tied to the mother but having to emulate the father who was basically hated, the son tended toward an exaggerated form of *machismo*, so very characteristic of those countries which have had the highest percentage of *mestizo* persons. Such a *machismo* in a *mestizo* society may be described as nothing but a sense of insecurity about one's own masculinity—an exaggeration of virility.

Identity with the despised mother is nowhere better illustrated than in the revolutionary battle cry: *Hijos de la chingada--que viva Mexico*[4] "Sons of the raped one—long live Mexico." The term *chingada* "one who is violated" is not the same as *puta* "prostitute"—one who gives herself voluntarily for gain. *Hijos de puta* is an expression of personal insult, but *Hijos de la chingada* became a symbol of common identity and revolt—identification with the submerged sector of society demanding its rights and ultimate control.

The attitude of the *conquistador* toward Indian women is not much different from the attitude of the young man in a better family toward the servant girl. He is biologically attracted but sociologically repelled. There is sexual attachment but social distance—and in this conflict many of the major tensions in Latin life arise. The child of such a union is naturally attached to the mother (for the father is largely irresponsible), but he hates the resulting status. At the same time, though emotionally attached to his mother, he tends to look down on her for permitting such abuse.[5]

This conflict becomes intensified by the manner in which legitimate children were reared in colonial times, for more often than not they were cared for almost entirely by Indian maids. It was the Indian woman who often nursed them, calmed their fears, wiped away their tears, and in a real sense loved them, while the actual mother often remained a distant and cold creature. The woman who provided the warmth of care was the socially despised person, and the woman who merely ordered people about was the highly esteemed person in the culture. Thus for many persons a gulf arose between sexual warmth and social acceptability, between real emotional security and behavioral acceptability.

This basic conflict between what was loved and what was respected has expressed itself in different attitudes toward female companionship. Often the wife became the symbol of the distant mother—idealized, respected, and almost "untouchable"—while the mistress or sweetheart became the symbol of real comfort and security but in association with a "despised class."[6] This emotional conflict has tended to develop two types of sexuality: one in relationship to the wife and another in relationship to the mistress. Toward the legal wife, sexuality takes on a characteristic "functional" aspect, for the wife is the maternal symbol—revered, delicate, beautiful, and religious. Toward the mistress, however, sexuality becomes highly sensuous, for the mistress is the symbol of security, warmth, affection, and sexual response.

Due to the conflict in loyalties, wives quite naturally reach out for security, but often they do not find this in their husbands, who are more or less expected to have affairs with other women. Having lost the exclusive attention of a husband, the wife tends to be quite possessive toward her sons.[7] But though the son feels very dependent upon his mother, he must nevertheless demonstrate a *machismo* spirit if he is to be accepted in the male world. Aniceto Aramoni insists that this conflict produces almost disastrous implications for the young man "who is faced with the mother figure, on whom he depends intensely and at the same time irrationally, and to whom he must prove his own masculine dominance with all its inherent implications."[8] Rogelio Díaz[9] contends that it is this type of love for the mother which really interferes with the son's capacity to love a wife in a wholly satisfactory way. The young man is thus faced with two rather tragic conflicts: first, a strong feeling of dependence upon the mother, while being constrained by the values of the male world to react against such a state, and second, an ideal conception of love within marriage, while experiencing real passion outside of marriage.

For the female child there is usually no other recourse than to play the role of passivity—to be dominated. But if she does not succeed by virtue of her personal appearance and sexuality to attract a male, there is very little opportunity for her, except in religion.

It is little wonder that such strong emotional conflicts, which tend to be highly oedipal, should give rise to serious tensions and psychoneuroses. Rogelio Díaz[10] insists that as a result of such conflicts there is a much greater tendency to hypochondria in Latin America than in North America. His studies over a period of 18 years in Mexico indicate that in the Mexican population some 32 percent of the males are neurotic and 44 percent of the females are similarly ill. Such psychosomatic illnesses as *susto* "fright," *descontento* "unhappiness," *higado* "liver," and *bilis* "bile," are suringly prevalent.[11]

Machismo expresses itself in a number of different ways,

which can generally be classed as attempts either to demonstrate sexual prowess or to show antagonism to females.
Sexual identification comes very early in life, and perhaps
the greatest insult to a small boy is to compare him to a
girl. Both Abelardo Villegas and Samuel Ramos describe
the exaggerated form of masculinity in boys as consisting of
(1) irritability, (2) a hostile spirit, (3) quarrelsomeness,
(4) demonstration of virility, (5) emphasis on the testicles,
and (6) phallic language and symbols.[12] A phrase such as
tiene huevos, literally "he has eggs," is not, however,
used merely to refer to the physical organs or to sexual
capacity. It is often employed in speaking of exceptional
bravery—a person who does not fear death. It can also
imply unusual intellectual capacity, especially in being able
to contrive new and valuable solutions in interpersonal
difficulties.[13]

Bragging about masculine sexuality is interpreted by some
as merely further proof of an inferiority complex and an
inability to achieve full satisfaction in sex.[14] Some of this
underlying inferiority seems also to express itself in a sense
of irresponsibility, for which the symbol of the cock is so
frequently employed—as, for example, in the folk song,
*Soy como el gallo, que tiene cincuenta y a ninguna la
mantiene* "I am like a cock who has fifty hens but doesn't
provide for any of them." María Elvira Bermúdez[15] contends
that this refusal to assume responsibility for educating and
caring for the children reflects a feeling that this would be
something too "feminine." So widespread is the pattern of
irresponsibility in Mexico City that of 3,000 children studied
by Dr. Bermúdez,[16] 10 percent were without any ties to either
father or mother and lived as vagabonds; 32 percent could
not give the name of the father; 11 percent had no father in the
home; 11 percent had no mother in the home (they were living
with relatives or friends); and 47 percent were illegitimate,
but with some association with mothers and fathers.[17]

John Mackay has described certain aspects of this emphasis upon *machismo* as three types or perversions of true
hombridad (masculinity): *El Don Juan, El Snob, and El
Ególatra* (worshiper of self).[18] These exaggerated manifestations of *machismo* only provide confirmation of the
importance attached to the dominance of the masculine role
in Latin society.

If the male is to overemphasize his own masculine role, it can only be done at the expense of the female role. But, as noted above, opposition to the female is a kind of two-edged sword—"a depreciation of the female, but living obsessed by women."[19] Such behavior may also be described as resulting from a simultaneous occurrence of a lack of real respect for women and an actual fear of them.[20] The very fact that they must be "conquered" and dominated indicates something of the latent fear which some Latin males have of women. Such a compulsion to demonstrate one's capacity to conquer can only reflect an underlying insecurity—as Aniceto Aramoni says, "In each person dominated by the *machismo* ideal there exists a profound and deep-rooted doubt as to his own real manliness, as far as women and other men are concerned."[21]

Popular views tend to corroborate these views of *machismo*. In popular ranchero music women are often praised for their beauty but are generally described as not to be trusted. They are like a mare which cannot be broken. The "bad woman" is either the one who cannot be broken or the one who is masculine, in the sense that she is aggressive, active (not passive), does not reveal herself, and loves and then abandons (rather than waiting to be abandoned).[22] The "good woman," however, must remain faithful to her lover, even though he may quickly tire of her, for her remaining faithful is a symbol of his own *machismo*,[23] well illustrated by a popular folk song:

> Vengo en busca de una ingrata
> De una joven presumida
> Que se fue con mi querer.
> Traigo ganas de encontrarla
> Pa' enseñarle que de un hombre
> No se burla una mujer.[24]

This song may be translated freely as: "I am going in search of a thankless and conceited young woman who has gone away with my love. I want to find her and teach her that no woman can make fun of a man."

The conflict in the values of *machismo* and *hembrismo* is also very evident in courtship, in which "love is conquest,"[25] a kind of conflict to penetrate the reality of the other person.

On this basis courtship is built on deceit and conflict,[26] for the woman conceives of her suitor instinctively as an enemy and of other women as competitors. Thus in Latin America the typical triangle has been two women and one man, whereas in North America the typical triangle has traditionally consisted of two men and one woman. But if courtship is regarded as hostility, then marriage is "the fall," and to this extent the man is victorious.[27]

Despite the fact that *hembrismo* calls for women to be passive, abnegating, long-suffering, and enduring, it would be a mistake to think that all Latin women are mere puppets or dolls. Quite the contrary! Latin women are often quite strong-willed and in many situations are aggressive, even within their ostensibly passive role. They manage to dominate, though usually not overtly. Their real power comes from their role in the family, for as the father tends to be irresponsible or as he may go off philandering, it is obviously the mother who becomes the emotional center of the family, the one who provides the security and permanence so indispensable to the continued meaning of the home. Moreover, she usually becomes the mediator between the authoritarian father and the children. Thus as emotional center and as intercessor the mother has a role which becomes focal, and her status is preserved by both laws and social pressures militating strongly against divorce. In a few instances a dominant role for certain women has actually been advocated. Santa Teresa insisted that the nuns of her order should be "not women but like strong men," so virile that they would startle people into action.[28] But this very plea is itself a confirmation of the typical role which women were expected to assume.

Some features of the *machismo-hembrismo* conflict may become somewhat clearer if one examines certain contrasts with North American patterns of life. For example, many North Americans regard courtship ideally as consisting of self-exposure rather than deception, for they are anxious to know whether they are really suited for one another. This does not mean that they refrain from premarital sexual relations any more than Latins do. It is only that sex takes on quite another meaning. It is not conquering or being conquered, but self-exposure with the hope of finding some degree of mutual fulfillment.

Similarly, within the home there are certain important contrasts between Latin America and North America. For example, in North America the father is much more likely to be weak and even bossed by his wife. Moreover, by not providing sons with a well-defined father or male role, he often leaves them in emotional doubt as to their own sexual identification—thus providing some basis for the much greater degree of homosexuality in North America than exists in Latin America. On the other hand, in relations with Latin American countries the United States has too often adopted a kind of father role—a "father-knows-best" attitude. This is naturally very much resented, for in view of certain basic distrust of the father role anyway, it is no wonder that this paternalizing attitude on the part of many North Americans tends to infuriate Latins.

Even concerning the role of the grandmother, Latins and North Americans tend to differ considerably as the result of the different ways in which diverse values motivate different kinds of behavior.[29] For example, in the United States grandmothers in the upper-middle and upper classes usually want to appear young and often travel extensively with their husbands—thus sharing in certain aspects or interests of his work. In Latin America, however, the grandmother is much more likely to try to assume some responsibility for the education or care of the grandchildren and as such to compete with her daughter, for her security is to be found in the mother role, not in the men's world.

Within the Evangelical community in Latin America, the tensions of *machismo* and *hembrismo* manifest themselves in ways which are typical of Latin American values. In the first place, there is a tendency (though perhaps less marked among Evangelicals than among Roman Catholics) for fathers to want to control the selection of husbands for their daughters. In the second place, there is a rather strong avoidance of discussion of sex within the church, especially among the more theologically conservative. In wanting to control the selection of a son-in-law, Evangelical men are only expressing a widespread Latin practice, but North American missionaries find this attitude hard to understand, for they assume that as a result of the gospel, which emphasizes the free choice of people in religious matters, there will also be an expression of free choice in the selection of a mate. The extent to which Evangelical fathers feel that they need scriptural backing for their decisive role in the selection of husbands for their daughters was well illustrated in the reaction of many pastors and laymen to the alternative interpretation of 1 Corinthians 7. 36-38. In traditional translations this passage indicated that it was up to the father to decide whether his virgin daughter should marry or remain single. With the suggestion, however, that this passage should be changed to indicate that it was the decision of the fiance as to whether the two should marry or remain single, there was a strong protest from many quarters, since such a revision seemed to undermine the authority of the Latin father and "to make him no different from a Yankee gringo," as one Latin expressed it.

It is also significant that, apart from some notable exceptions, sexual problems and differences of values are rarely discussed in Evangelical churches. In some measure this is part of the widespread view that sex and religion are in quite different worlds. Evangelicals have come to deal quite openly and objectively with many burning issues in Hispanoamerican life, but for the most part sex is not one of these. Perhaps the real reason is that there are such ambivalent attitudes concerning sex and such wide differences between ideal and real behavior. The fact that much of sexual behavior is covert rather than overt means that people are quite hesitant to discuss it. In considerable measure this is also true of theologically conservative Protestant churches in North America, but increasingly less so as greater freedom of discussion and more openness are encouraged. However, to expose oneself is not Latin, and Latins are particularly hesitant to expose themselves about such ambivalent problems within a context which seems utterly divorced from sex; and religious activity is usually looked upon as such a context.

Society

On the social level *machismo* expresses itself in a variety of ways. *Machismo* becomes a form of violent aggressiveness, often assuming the form of murder. In Latin America murders are far more "crimes of passion" than calculated attempts to liquidate an opposing gang. There are, of course,

feuds over land and control of access, which may be
exceedingly costly in lives, and these conflicts may be
only projections of the aggressiveness of certain strong
leaders, in the same way that Latin revolutions often reflect
an aggressive *machismo*.

Another social aspect of *machismo* is the strong judgment
against homosexuality, especially in the passive role.
Anything effeminate about a man is not only laughed at by
other men but is equally scorned by women. Though there
may be a good deal of latent homosexuality in the Latin
world, it certainly is not expressed to the extent that it
is in North America, for strong emphasis on virility and
masculine dominance suppresses it.

Adult men are not the only ones who express aggressiveness against society. Gangs of young boys often show their
aggression. Without a responsible father figure, these
young boys express their aggressiveness by strong emphasis
on *machismo* values, through robbing, thieving, Don Juan
escapades, and taunting and escaping from authorities.[30]

Agressiveness is also widely shown in speech by loud
arguments and by humor based on exaggeration and absurdi-
ties. A phrase such as *curar el dolor de cabeza vaciando
la pistola en el cráneo* "curing a headache by emptying a
pistol into his skull" is typical of such braggadocio and
exaggerated use of language.[31]

Agressiveness toward women is obviously based on a
double standard, for the conqueror becomes confirmed in
his ability to conquer but he is never regarded as debased
by the object he conquers. This double standard reflects
the ancient idea that a fountain which pours water into a
dirty basin is not contaminated, while a vessel once filled
with dirty water will always remain contaminated.

Still another aspect of this aggressiveness is that males
frequently seem to prefer the companionship of other males
rather than of females. This helps to explain the tendency
for Latin males to congregate in bars, coffeehouses, and
places of recreation. They seem to be uneasy in the company
of women unless they are fully dominant. Moreover, among
males they can brag of their exploits without the danger of
being exposed. Part of the insecurity in this relationship
with females is to be found in the tendency for many Latins
to regard an ideal marriage as one in which the wife does not

have too much education—the adage: *Cuánto menos notable
sea, tánto mejor para la buena marcha del matrimonio*
"The less distinguished she (the wife) is, the better are the
chances of a successful marriage."[32] Under such circumstances the wife poses fewer threats to the man. Moreover,
in the *machismo* pattern it is not the wife who provides the
companionship, but the children and the home, and for this
purpose education for the wife is not an indispensable feature.

But *machismo* also leads to isolation. The man cannot
expose himself, for this would be to admit the degree of
ambivalence which underlies this pattern of behavior and
these combinations of values. He cannot confess his real
problems, for to do so would be to have his dominant role
exposed and his weakness made evident. He certainly cannot
afford to confess this to a woman, for then he would have
reversed roles and would no longer be a man sociologically.
His only possible confession can be to a Roman Catholic
priest, who stands outside of this male-female antithesis.

Contrasts between Latin America and North America at
this point of the social implications of *machismo* are
primarily in the extent of homosexuality. Many psychologists
have contended that because of poorly defined male roles in
American life, there is a great deal of homosexuality.
The fact that young boys are often raised so completely in
the feminine surroundings of the home and classroom
means that they frequently imbibe female rather than male
values. This seems to be particularly true in households in
which the mother dominates the father.

Traditionally, the emphasis on the male role has meant
that women have been kept somewhat in the background of
Latin life—in the home and in social situations. This,
however, is changing rapidly. With greater emphasis on
education of women and the increased participation of women
in business, *machismo* cannot express itself in the traditional
forms which confined women to a relatively narrow existence.

It is true that a North American is much more likely to
invite business friends to his home. In Latin America the
home is the symbol of the wife's precinct, where a man
relates to wife and children but not to people in general. A
Latin is much more likely to entertain in a restaurant or
hotel than in his home, for it is felt that bringing only
casual friends to one's home tends to violate the "holy

precinct," to expose the personal, untouchable aspect of
a man's life to the world.

In the Evangelical community in Latin America the
machismo - hembrismo tensions have manifested themselves
in several significant ways. In the first place, Latin men
have strongly resented taking orders from North American
women missionaries, some of whom are anything but
feminine either in appearance or in manner. Having not
been sufficiently feminine to attract a man within their own
culture, they have not infrequently overdeveloped their
nonfeminine characteristics, to the point of making themselves very difficult to comprehend socially.

At the same time there are some very strong-willed
Latin women in some indigenous Evangelical movements
in Latin America. In general, however, these women act
through some man: a nephew, an uncle, or a brother.
In this way they maintain a male front and therefore do not
create such a problem for the men whom they seek to
influence. When such women do not follow this pattern of
using a male front, they usually constitute very serious
problems.

As has been noted before, mission-sponsored Evangelical
churches in Latin America have often not attracted strong
Latin personalities. Too much domination from outside
and too little opportunity for independence of judgment
and action have discouraged potential leaders. This is
particularly true in situations in which missions succeeded
in training only "followership" rather than leadership,
for they gave rewards to whose who provided the "desired"
answers, not necessarily to those who provided the right
answers. In contrast with this, the indigenous Evangelical
churches have a number of very strong personalities
associated with them—men who were no doubt attracted
by the independence of such movements and who were also
strengthened in their inherent capacities by the nature of
their responsibilities.

Religion

It might even appear strange to think that a sexual
antagonism such as *machismo* and *hembrismo* would be in
any way related to religious expression, and yet it is perhaps

in the area of religion that these two tendencies have some of their greatest significance for Latin life and understanding of values.

On the supernatural level, *machismo* reinforces the Latin view of God as the *paterfamilias*, or dominant figure, demanding obedience and carrying out judgment or punishment. In traditional forms of religious expression, there is very little emphasis on the love of God, for this seems to be incompatible with customary beliefs about God's role. But in indigenous Pentecostalism, one frequently encounters the emphasis on *Dios es amor* "God is love." For these persons this has been the startling Good News which has changed their whole idea about God and how he relates himself to man.

The figure of Christ has traditionally been a symbol either of death or of a small child dependent on the care of his mother. As a symbol of death he fails to elicit continual identification, and as a child he tends rather to focus emotional response to his mother, the Virgin, who cares for him and by implication is prepared to care for all believers.

It is no wonder, therefore, that the Mary symbol has become a psychological necessity within the Roman Church, as noted in our chapter on Mariology, for people must have a symbol of life and beneficence, a mother mediatrix between needy people and a fearsome Father God—a reflection of the role of the Latin mother as intercessor between her children and their stern father.

On the human level, the Roman priest fulfills an ambivalent role. Before the altar he is the sacred Christ, but in the street he is a man. But in the area of *machismo* and *hembrismo*, he fills the role of "the third sex." His rejection of marriage is generally interpreted as implying that sex is somewhat bad—at least it is not fitting for sacred personages. A rather notable cardinal in Brazil used to refuse even to sleep in a room in which a married couple had ever slept, for he did not want to be contaminated by sex. This means that sex in marriage becomes relegated to the class of the less than perfect—even if not to the essentially and inherently bad. As such, however, it makes "ideal marriage" something so "sacred" as to interfere with its real sexual significance. Real sexual satisfaction is thus difficult to experience, since people cannot give themselves fully and wholly to one another. A kind of religiously imposed taboo comes between.

On the other hand, religion does tend to be identified with the feminine role, even as the garment of the priest is interpreted as symbolic of transvestism. The dominant role of traditional Roman Catholicism in Latin America is hence the female symbol of the mediating Virgin, not the masculine symbol of the living Christ. Moreover, the Church has its greatest appeal to women, who find security in its opposition to divorce and the opportunity for self-expression in an area of life which poses no threat to their interpersonal relations.

It is not without interest that in Latin America men tend to be strongly anticlerical, not merely because the Church seems to compete with their authority but also because it is essentially a feminine institution. So much is this the case that many men think that only men without manliness enter the priesthood—as an escape from the masculine role.

The *hembrismo* in Latin life quite inevitably expresses itself in Roman Catholic forms. In the supernatural area, it is the symbol of the Virgin, as the object of beauty, life, and tenderness. She must also be the inviolate, perpetually a virgin, the sinlessly immaculate. Only then, as the unconquered, can she become the ideal—the symbol of the eternal mother, with her central mediating role.

On the human level, the celibacy of priesthood also symbolizes something of the importance of the female role. Marriage would in fact be a kind of infidelity to the female deity, a betrayal of loyalty. In this connection it is not without significance that celibacy occurs primarily in those religions in which female deities are dominant or in situations in which the divine symbols may have been feminized, as in the case of the sexually ambivalent Buddhas.

For the laity the particular Virgin of the land rapidly becomes the symbol for that country, for this is the "earth mother." Not only may each country have its patron Virgin, but even rival groups may carry the emblems of different Virgins to symbolize their ethnic origins and partisan causes. In the War of Independence in Mexico, the blond Virgin of the Remedies became the symbol of the royalists, while the brown Virgin of Guadalupe became the rallying symbol of the insurgents. So intense became the identification that royalist soldiers would even shoot at images or pictures of the Virgin of Guadalupe as a means of damaging the cause of the rebellious *criollos* and *mestizos*.

The Virgin also becomes the symbol of solace for women—the symbol of the ideal mother, who bears children without having been conquered. The Virgin also symbolizes an emotional attachment to her Son, Jesus Christ, and not to her husband, even as the Latin mother expresses some of her deepest attachment to her own loyal son, and not to her wayward husband. Moreover, as symbolized in the Virgin, she is also the special choice of God, exalted above other women.

For men the Virgin becomes an identification with their own mother, the intercessor with the stern Father, and the emotional focus of the security of the home, for the mother always remains the faithful, suffering one. It is not without importance that in discussions with most Latins one can readily challenge almost any doctrine of the Roman Catholic Church without producing any special reaction, but even persons who are strongly anticlerical often react almost violently to any statement which seems to belittle the role of the Virgin. Santiago Ramírez[33] describes a gang of boys in Mexico City who lived together in a shack and who each night robbed drunks (despised father figures) but who always kept a candle burning in front of a small altar dedicated to the Virgin of Guadalupe, the symbol of "the Inviolate Mother."

One of the significant contrasts between Latin America and North America is the manner in which religion becomes identified with one or another parent. In Latin America one almost inevitably speaks of *la religión de mi madre* "the religion of my mother." This is the instinctive manner in which one identifies himself with his religious tradition. In contrast with this, a North American will most often speak of "the faith of our fathers." Here religion becomes an expression of quite a different familial background.

Within the Evangelical Church in Latin America there has been a strong reaction against the traditional role of the Virgin, for quite instinctively Protestants have sensed that here is the crucial difference. Having refused this female symbol of beauty, warmth, and love, Protestants have emphasized much more the love of God and the victorious Christ, key themes in many of the indigenous Evangelical churches in Latin America. If the gospel is to be Good News, it must be presented in terms of the Christ who loves everyone, but this Christ must not be effeminate—a kind of bearded lady in a nightgown.

Philosophy

In the popular world view, *machismo* is a justified expression of the "order of things," in which some few persons command (the active role) and the rest obey (the passive role). The one who commands does not, of course, work with his hands, for this would betray his servant (or even "female") status. Thus it is that those who obey are the ones who must work—as a symbol of their servant position.

This also means that the one who commands is expected to have a plurality of contacts, to move freely in the world of men and things. He therefore is expected to have more than one job, for a single job cannot possibly demand all of his energy or give him the opportunity to display the total creativity of which he is capable. Just as the "leader" in life cannot be expected to remain faithful to a single woman, so the intellectual leader can scarcely be expected to follow a single profession. Rather than being devoted to one goal, one must show capacity to conquer several.

Machismo becomes rather instinctively a justification for a double moral standard, which though seldom openly espoused is nevertheless privately and consistently held. The *machismo-hembrismo* dichotomy also produces a strict division of labor, and with little or no possibility for the confusion of roles. Only in recent times has this division been seriously challenged.

But when the *machismo-hembrismo* contrast is raised to the level of a popular philosophy, lack of sexual fulfillment becomes almost a disgrace for a Latin man or woman. For the male, there is lack of proper self-expression. In this respect he has somehow cheated the world of his potentiality. For the woman, lack of sexual fulfillment is practically immoral, for she has deprived someone of his rights to self-expression.

In this area of popular philosophy, the *machismo-hembrismo* distinction becomes a source of quite important contrasts between North American and Latin American ways of life. In North America the boss usually does not hesitate to pitch in to help get the job done, and the engineer is not reluctant to get his hands dirty—something quite unthinkable in traditional Latin society, although now finding more and more acceptance in the technological middle class. The North American experiences a good deal less division of labor between men and women. Especially in the upper classes in American life, men are much more likely to help their wives with the dishes or other housework. Since there is greater reciprocity, there is also greater justification for sharing duties.

Though Latins may look upon lack of sexual fulfillment as being somehow morally wrong, the North American is likely to view such lack of fulfillment as representing a type of neurotic aberration, something strange but not necessarily wrong. A part of his Puritan ethic remains with him, and chastity cannot be regarded as morally wrong, even though it may be thought of as socially and psychologically abnormal.

Within the Evangelical community in Latin America, the new outlook upon interpersonal relationships, especially within the nuclear family, tends to produce more unity and less tension, for there is a greater degree of mutuality, greater reciprocity, and more confidence and trust. These biblically based values become high priority factors among Evangelicals, who often practice considerable openness with one another. Thus people are not under the former pressures to defend themselves from penetration.

On the other hand, there is a tendency for the Evangelical pastor to assume quite an ideal view, to insist on telling others what they should do, without pitching in and doing it himself. Such professionalism is understandable within the context of a tradition which makes such a distinction between those who command and those who obey.

Aesthetics

Though all persons who have studied Latin life have been curiously and intriguingly aware of the importance of the *machismo-hembrismo* contrast as it influences Latin art and architecture, it is not easy to describe such developments, for truly creative Latin art is highly personal and subliminal in its implications. As pointed out in previous sections, the way in which the contrasts authoritarianism-individualism and idealism-realism affect and influence aesthetic expression can be rather easily described and documented. But for something as "internal" as sexual conflict one cannot be dogmatic, nor does one see the symbolic evidence of such contrasts in constant display.

In popular art, the phallic symbol of the clenched fist with the extended second finger is too obvious to go unnoted, and frequent use of the sun and moon (coming from Indian as well as medieval European motifs) exhibits some of this same aesthetic awareness of the machismo-hembrismo tensions.

Yet perhaps more important than the symbolism in Latin American art are the themes themselves, for where Latins are truly creative they have generally depicted struggle. This has not been restricted to portraying historic movements and battles but has involved man's struggle against the machine, his battle against oppression, his conflict with political enslavement, and his passion for intellectual freedom. The great Mexican muralists have been propagandists armed with brushes rather than with pens. They have not been content to decorate space with paint but have communicated a revolutionary message by means of design.

Politics

The true expression of *machismo* on the part of the political leader is to be wholly and completely male. Political candidates are often pictured in Latin America with "bull necks"—symbols of their masculinity. Some of the most romantic leaders have been persons like Pancho Villa, whose fighting has been interpreted by many as being in large measure only a projection of his own *machismo* and whose personal life was one constant series of amorous exploits designed to display his capacities.

Machismo has also contributed to the generational conflict in Latin life. Not all the violence of youth against the older generation can be explained merely by the revolt of individualism against authority. It has much deeper roots, for in the revolt against authority youth are also bent on demonstrating their own *machismo* —the symbol of their adulthood. The one uncontrovertible way to demonstrate one's own power is to take power away from those who have had it in the past. Thus revolt serves not only to express the attack of individualism against authoritarianism but also to demonstrate the *machismo* of those who are seeking adult status in opposition to those whose powers are suspected of being on the wane.

In North America the tendency is to depict political leaders as being "human"—just like everyone else. Only in this way, so the publicists say, will the masses identify with the leader and vote for him. In Latin America this is not the normal procedure. The leader is chosen by the people precisely because he is not like everyone else. When some journalists and photographers from the United States interviewed former Mexican President Lázaro Cárdenas on one occasion, they tried to get him to let them take pictures of him eating his lunch, shaving, and relaxing after a day's work. They insisted that they wanted to "humanize" this man who had been so strong as to nationalize the oil industry in Mexico and thus force out of operation a number of American companies. But President Cárdenas was simply not interested in being humanized. As president of a sovereign state he had no intention of exposing himself to an American public that wanted to think of him as just another man, for he was not just another man. He was a leader, and as such he was different.

A summary of Latin American characteristics

Though we have mentioned a number of Latin American characteristics in contrast with North American ones, these can probably be best summarized in terms of the following ways in which North Americans would characterize Latins: proud (to the point of arrogance), aggressive (desirous of dominating), passionate, and volatile (subject to unpredictable change). As has been noted from a number of quotations from Latin authors, there would be substantial agreement on these matters among Latin American investigators as well. But what North Americans often overlook is that these same characteristics also contain certain very important positive values. In a sense, Latins are justifiably proud. They not only have something to be proud of in their heritage and accomplishments, but the right amount of pride can be an important main-spring to creative action. The characteristic of aggressiveness may also be of positive value in releasing the dynamic energy so characteristic of the creative explosiveness of Latin life. Passionateness provides a warmth and feeling in Latin life which makes it much more meaningful and living than the cold, calculating quality of corporate efficiency in North American behavior. Similarly, the volatile quality of Latin life can also be a trigger to touch off unsuspected human energies when directed to creative enterprise.

Taken together, these qualities of pride, aggression, passion, and volatility have produced a number of most important results: intense creativity in many forms of art, music, and literature; a deep love of beauty; an unusual capacity for friendship; brilliant philosophical insights; inspiring religious devotion; and some of the most colorful behavior to be found in the world.

By way of contrast, Latins see North Americans as symbols of cultural mediocrity (in which money is regarded as more important than manners and cash more valuable than culture), mechanical impersonalism (in which men not only glory in machines but become increasingly like them), and materialism (in which men are not only ranked on the basis of their incomes, but in which somehow these riches are equated with blessings from God). The Latin may be blatantly materialistic, but he is rarely deluded into thinking that his riches are a sign of divine blessing, as is the case with the "Protestant ethic." A Latin may worship Mammon, but when he does, he usually does not delude himself into thinking that he is really worshiping God.

Latin society in contrast with Indian societies

It is most difficult to speak in general terms of Indian societies in Latin America, for there are more than 200 Indian groups, of quite different types. First, there are the so-called peasant groups, such as the Quechuas and Aymaras of the Andean highlands, who have been economically enslaved and partially "civilized," in the sense that they have been made completely dependent upon the dominant society. These persons either work as peons on the farms of great landowners or possess their own lands in isolated areas. Second, there are the marginal groups, such as the San Blas of Panama and the Yaquis of Mexico, who maintain their own tribal structures but who are economically quite dependent upon the dominant society. Third, there are the primitive groups, who still live as independent bands in remote regions of the largely impenetrable jungles.

Indian groups are at various stages of crisis, demoralization, reorientation, and reintegration, and in some situations the position of individuals is extremely ambivalent. In Mexico an Indian may be a part of both cultures if he wishes, for he may move back and forth between the Indian and Mexican ways of life—in a sense he may become bicultural. In Peru, however, he must either be an Indian or a *ladino* (i.e. *civilizado*), and to be the latter he usually has to move away from the place where he lived as an Indian.

Despite the many striking differences in Indian life, especially in the so-called peasant societies, there are certain very important ways in which Indians differ from Latins in their outlook, and these may be conveniently described in terms of the very contrasts which have been used to indicate certain fundamental features of Latin values. In the first place, there is very little conflict between authoritarianism and individualism in Indian society, for life is simply not structured in terms of a pyramid, with a few people commanding the rest. Rather, life may be regarded more as a ladder, with people climbing up to different levels of authority and with responsibilities matching each successive level of authority. Furthermore, the fiesta is not a revolution for the Indian but an ecstasy, an escape from the routine slavery of his peonage. Physical work is not only a normal form of life for all levels but is completely honorable.

The Indian is not in conflict because of tensions between the ideal and the real, for he lives close to the realities of his existence. Though he may accept the statue of the Virgin as a "god" who insures rain, this idealism does not prevent him from a realistic appraisal of the Virgin's capacities. If she does not produce rain, he is very likely to throw out the image or even to whip it in public.

At the same time, most Indians avoid some of the problems inherent in wide divisions between ideal and real behavior by rejecting deceptive symbolizations. For example, he rarely gives a high priority to conspicuous consumption, except, of course, in the ecstasy of fiestas.

Most Indians are not bothered by the *machismo-hembrismo* tension, for marriage involves continuous interdependence of complementary roles. Moreover, marriage itself is looked upon as economic cooperation more than as sexual conquest, and hence there is little reason for tensions of the Latin type to develop. Indian men generally assume their fair share of responsibility toward the family, and thus there is usually an adequate father figure for the children.

In the area of sexual symbolism, most Indians emphasize fertility, not aggression. The meaning of sex is describable more in terms of the processes of nature than of a conflict between human beings.

Due to the special circumstances under which the peasant-type Indians have had to live during the centuries, it is quite understandable that they should seem withdrawn, resistant, and defensive. Had they not been so, they would have been overrun long ago. Only by withdrawing could they possibly protect themselves from the overwhelming economic and social pressures of the technologically superior culture. At the same time, the Indian way of life has been very largely static. This is not, however, the result of laziness but of an attempt to preserve the balance in nature and between people. One must not scratch the belly of mother earth too deeply, or destroy the protecting humus compost that lies rotting about, or dig out the trickling spring, for to violate nature is to destroy her capacity to continue nourishing the people who are dependent on her. Thus one does not conquer nature or exploit it. Rather, one must work carefully with nature, lest the spirits be angry and the fields no longer produce.

The Indian has also developed, as a means of self-preservation, a kind of double orientation. He has acquired two faces in social relations: one stolid, uncommunicating face which he wears in relationships with members of the dominant *ladino* culture, and another friendly, open face which he wears in relationships to Indians of the same in-group. Similarly, his religion has two quite distinct theological levels. In the upper "Christian" level he conforms to the outward forms of ritual observance, which make most chance observers think he is piously Roman Catholic. But the lower level of his religion (the lower story of his theological house, and the one in which he lives most of the time) is thoroughly indigenous. The words of the prayers may come from the missal, but the deities to whom they are addressed are often the gods of the volcanoes.

Evaluations

Even when differences between cultures have been described with all the possible objectivity that one can employ, it is still inevitable that judgments and evaluations will be involved, despite most energetic attempts to avoid them. Moreover, evaluations will almost inevitably reflect the cultural heritage of which one is a part. It is for this very reason that we have attempted to highlight differences between Latin and North American values in terms of the typical ways in which such peoples view one another.

But in any ultimate judgment on related values in corresponding cultures, there is simply no set of values or any scheme of evaluations that can claim a universal or even general validity. Preferences are largely a matter of personal reactions, based upon all the prejudices and partial knowledge to which we all as human beings are restricted. Actually, it is quite unfair to try to weigh different total cultures in the balances in order to assign relative ranks or values to them. Who could possibly assign numerical values to qualities such as friendship in contrast with efficiency, beauty in opposition to cleanliness, and creativity as opposed to discipline? Such values are simply not commensurate.

Moreover, the true meaning or significance of differences in cultures is to be found largely in their very diversity. If we are to live fully and meaningfully in a world of plural cultures, we must learn not only to respect these differences but to enjoy them, not only to study them but to receive enriching experiences as the result of contacts with their representatives. It is only in this way that North Americans and Latin Americans can enrich one another—by mutual contact and reciprocal sharing. To do this, one must recognize his own roots within his own culture, his own basis of understanding, and the values which tend to influence him so greatly. He must not be so enamored with the out-group (the other society) that he loses perspective in judging fairly the failures and successes of his own heritage.

In conclusion, we must return to a theme suggested in the first chapter of Part I, namely, the wide diversity in individual conduct and values. Though we have inevitably been forced to deal in broad generalizations (which compound insights and distortions), it is still essential to recognize, first, that what unites people in a common bond of humanity is much greater than that which separates them into different cultures; and second, that within each large cultural grouping the differences between individuals are much greater than the diversities noted between the different cultures. Nevertheless, it is on the basis of the broad general system of values that we can judge individual variation, and it is by using these general values that we can help to understand behavior which differs radically from our own. Only in this way can we comprehend the patterns of life of others and begin to judge meaningfully the ways in which we ourselves customarily think and live.

Part II

Background
and Developments

5
Social Structure and Evangelism[1]

For many years those concerned with the problems of
evangelism in Latin America have been keenly aware of
some of the significant correlations between different
social structures and the diversities of response to the
gospel. For one thing, relatively few people from the upper
classes and not very many from the middle class ever become
associated with Evangelical churches. This has meant that
the membership of most of the Protestant churches has
come from the upper brackets of the lower class. The leadership within these churches has seemed to come primarily
from the families of independent tradesmen and merchants,
e.g. carpenters, shoemakers, blacksmiths, and shopkeepers.
It would appear that the gospel has had an attraction for just
those groups which had much to gain, e.g. education for
their children, a sense of importance (as colaborers with
God in the Kingdom of Heaven), and recompense for having
been so largely excluded from the upper brackets of Latin
American society, which tradition has identified with
Roman Catholicism. Conversely, these same people had
very little to lose by becoming Protestants. They were not
so likely to lose their jobs, were not dependent upon some
one person for their social and economic security (as in
the case of the day laborer or peon), and were never
cultivated to any great extent by the Roman Church, which

traditionally concentrated most of its attention upon the elite classes.

The phenomenal growth of the Pentecostal movement among the people of Latin America has served to highlight the relationship of social classes to the communication of the gospel, for not only is the Pentecostal movement as large as all the other Protestant denominations put together, but it has had success not only among the lower classes, from which its membership is largely drawn, but also among some of the upper classes.

Furthermore, missionaries (both Protestant and Roman Catholic) have been quick to note that it is always so much easier to begin work in new towns or recently built communities than in areas where people have lived for a long time. All of these facts have served to focus our attention on the possibilities of understanding more adequately some of the fundamental problems of social structure in Latin America and their bearing on the task of evangelism.

Acute problems in evangelism

On almost every hand the average missionary faces certain acute problems in evangelism, and a number of these seem to be directly related to factors in social structure. For example, not infrequently churches have flourished and grown for a period of five to ten years, only to be followed by twenty years of almost complete stagnation. Such churches seem to have reached a particular group within a community and then to have stopped growing. In some instances a few persons are won to the gospel in the initial attempts to start a new church, but their very presence in the church seems to prevent the entrance of others. In other churches the social standing of the members rises rapidly through improved education, greater ambition, and the indirect results of a higher sense of responsibility—characteristics which lead to greater financial rewards. However, the tendency is for such churches to lose touch with the very classes from which most of the members originally came.

A particularly difficult problem exists in Protestant churches in which there is a class cleavage within the church itself. In one church in Cuba there is a morning congregation composed primarily of upper-middle class young people, many of whom have a university education. The evening congregation consists of older people from the lower-middle and upper-lower classes. The rivalry between such groups in all phases of the church life is pathetic, for it hampers the potential ministry of the entire group and robs the people of a true sense of fellowship.

The difference of response between people in small rural communities and those in the cities has always called for certain adaptations in missionary approach, but the basic problems become increasingly more acute as churches in the urban centers assume responsibility for work in rural areas. Quite often they fail completely to establish a really vital work in which the rural people feel anything more than a kind of "poor country cousin" relationship to the city congregation. This distinction of class levels becomes even more difficult in a divided society, one made up of a Spanish and Indian constituency. The Indians are usually left out, not because the Spanish-speaking people purposely thrust them aside, but simply because they do not understand the means by which a vigorous Indian constituency may be developed.

The role of schools

In the early years of Protestant missionary work in Latin America, the establishment of schools, both primary and secondary, was supposed to be a major factor in overcoming certain of the major difficulties inherent in the social structure. These schools were not only supposed to educate the children of Evangelicals, but were calculated to create among non-Evangelicals a favorable attitude toward the Evangelical cause. Some schools have largely fulfilled this purpose, but a number have singularly failed. By an essentially secular viewpoint these schools have educated certain people away from the Evangelical community and have often failed to bring into that community those from the outside who might have special talents or abilities. The so-called neutralist view of many Evangelical schools is well illustrated by the recent boast of the principal of one of the largest mission schools of Latin America, who insisted that during the last 11 years of the school's existence not one student had been "converted."

In view of the numerous problems posed by various factors in the social structure of Latin society, certain questions are crucial: What is the basic class structure of these societies? What explains the acceptance of the gospel by one group and not by others? What are the forces and techniques of social change? How do people change their class status within Latin American society? What bearing has the proclamation of the gospel on such changes? What should be the basic strategy in approaching Latin society?

The structure of Latin American society

The structure of society in Latin America is highly complex and differs considerably from area to area. However, despite the possibility of a certain amount of error resulting from oversimplification, one can describe certain essential characteristics of Latin American society by means of a type of inverted jewel diamond diagram:

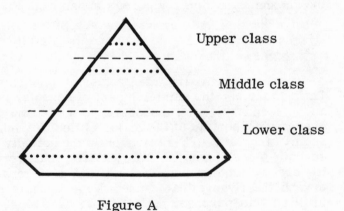

Figure A

Figure A symbolizes what are probably the major characteristics of most societies in Latin America, in which the narrow point represents the elite, the central portion the middle class, and the base portion the lower class. The upper class is generally divisible into two subclasses: (1) the old families, representing the traditional aristocracy, and (2) the *nouveaux riches*, those who have only recently acquired wealth and prestige. Some very rich people in the lower-upper class may be accepted into the upper-upper class, if they have some special influence or political power, but in general the two layers of elite are rather well defined.

The middle class is similarly divided between (1) the upper-middle class, consisting of successful but not so wealthy professionals such as doctors, lawyers, professors, politicians, engineers, and businessmen; and (2) the lower-middle class, consisting of white-collar workers such as clerks, bookkeepers, technicians, small business-men, and schoolteachers.

The lower class is divided between (1) the upper-lower class, made up of less prosperous tradesmen, factory workers, independent small farmers, domestic workers, and day laborers; and (2) the lower-lower class, consisting of the extremely poor seasonal workers, indigent share-croppers, and the habitually unemployed.

We must not assume that Figure A reflects accurately the actual proportion of the respective population, for the relative size of the various classes differs greatly in the various countries. We do not have the statistics necessary to produce a thoroughly accurate picture of the various societies, but we can approximate something of the diversity in types in the following diagrams, designed to portray Haitian, Uruguayan, and Peruvian societies:

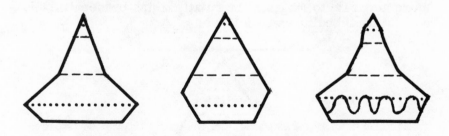

I. Haitian Society II. Uruguayan Society III. Peruvian Society

Figure B

There are several significant features of the diagrams in Figure B. Diagram I has a definite constriction between the class one elite and the class two elite, a distinction which is fully recognized by the Haitians themselves and a boundary which is as difficult to pass over as any other in the social structure. The Haitian middle class is also quite restricted, and the lower class is largest at near the lowest level.

In Uruguayan society, the middle class is not only relatively large, but the transition from the lower class and into the upper class is not so pronounced as in the case of Haiti. Moreover, the number of people who are indigent is not as great as in Haiti, hence the narrower base.

In Peruvian society, the middle class is proportionately less than in Uruguayan society, with a gradual transition from the upper-lower class, but the society bulges in the lower portions of the upper-lower class. In Diagram III, moreover, there is an additional feature, namely, the wavy solid line which marks the division between the predominantly Indian population (classified roughly on the basis of habitual use of an Indian language and the wearing of Indian-type clothing) and the Spanish-speaking people. The Indian population is the lowest in the social structure as far as general prestige is concerned, but some members of this class reach up into the upper-lower class. However, if they are to go up very far, they must adopt the classificatory symbols of the dominant group, namely, Spanish language and "Western" dress.

In the case of Peruvian society, it would probably be more accurate to diagram the relationships between the two coexisting subcultures as follows:

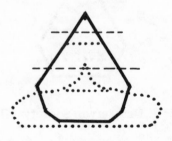

Figure C

In this structure an individual may possess a double status. For example, he may be in the elite within the Indian society, but only in the upper-lower class or lower-middle class of the non-Indian society. However, it would be a serious mistake to assume that the social role of Indians within the Indian community can be determined by any general classification of the Indian within the composite national structure.

This same principle of multiple classification may apply to any subculture or dependent social group. For example, in a small rural area the local elite may rate as only upper-middle class in the society of the nearby town and as lower-middle class in the still more inclusive structure of the nation.

Bases of class structure

From this description of the different social classes, one could presume that wealth would be the primary criterion of class membership. There is no denying the importance of money, but it is certainly not the only factor, or even the principal one, at least not for certain divisions. For example, some members of the first-class elite (the upper-upper class) are often less wealthy than many persons in the second-class elite (the lower-upper class). In fact, the "aristocracy," which often prides itself on being a class set apart by blood descent, spurns the criterion of money as a culturally inferior basis of ascertaining "human worth." The position of the Roman Catholic clergy also contradicts the criterion of wealth, for priests from relatively low classes are accepted into the upper brackets despite their lack of personal wealth, but they are usually never admitted into the highest class, unless a papal appointment to the hierarchy overrides local class structures. Persons with exceptional talents, (e.g. artists, singers, and dancers), or those with gifted intellects (e.g. writers, professors, and orators), may be admitted to a class which for the most part consists of considerably more wealthy members.

Class membership is not simply a matter of wealth or of family lineage or of special talents. It includes all of these plus political influence, leadership ability, and the favor of influential friends.

In speaking about social classes, one tends to get the impression that the distinctions are perfectly obvious to everyone, including the members of the society in question. However, these class distinctions are not fully evident, since people do not wear labels. Nevertheless, people in Latin America are quite conscious of the class to which they belong. This is much less true of people in the United States, where the classes are less well defined, where people are supposed to deny the existence of classes, and where most people insist that they belong to the middle class. The classes in Latin America can, however, be delineated without too much trouble by determining those groups which (1) participate together in social functions, (2) tend to intermarry, and (3) recognize their essential identity of outlook and mutual interests. Furthermore, each class is aware that those "above" have greater prestige and those "below" have less. Accordingly, people in all classes, except those at the top, tend to want to climb up in the scale of prestige.

What we have described as the different social classes are essentially prestige classes. There is no inherent reason why certain groups should be granted more prestige than others (other societies in the world have quite different prestige systems), but the Latin American societies do possess their typical structure, and one must reckon with it.

In describing classes as "lower" and "higher," we only have reference to the built-in prestige factors. Certainly such terms as "higher" and "lower" must not be interpreted as representing any moral evaluation, though that is what many members of the upper classes would like to have others think. If we were to judge the social classes on the basis of such criteria as honesty, reliability, sense of responsibility to family, hospitality, and willingness to sacrifice for the sake of the community, it is quite likely that in many instances the upper-lower class and the lower-middle class would come out on top. This division of social classes and their scaling from high to low is based essentially on one principle, namely, the degree of prestige which the members of a society associate with the respective classes.

In speaking of prestige as a determinant of classes, we recognize that the pattern is not one of absolute grades and fixed boundaries. That is to say, the classes of Latin American society are not castes, as in India. Rather, they are somewhat fluid groupings of people who associate together in various ways and who recognize in some measure the equality of their status. Prestige, therefore, is a polar element easily recognizable in the extremes but less obvious in the central zones. Moreover, within the six classes which constitute the major divisions recognizable in Latin life there are numerous minor scales of prestige.

Orientation of classes

The orientation of most members of all but the highest class is upward. That is to say, most people want to have more prestige. A number of people in the lowest classes have seemed to be largely resigned to their status, but within the last few years the development of leftist labor movements in Latin America has resulted in a widespread concern for upward drive among the lowest class.

Most members of the highest class are relatively content with their lot. Their only concern seems to be the preservation of the status quo. Hence, they are skeptical of any radical changes and unwilling to make room for many competitors in their class. In fact, any major assault on their class of top elite by the "newly rich" is usually resisted vigorously with all the snobbery of which this snob-conscious class is capable.

The pressures for change of class status are strongest in the rising elements of the middle class, but liberal political ideas have also induced major segments of the lower class to believe that what they would like, namely, more prestige and a greater share in material rewards, are not only desirable but attainable, and if not by their own personal efforts then by means of political revolution. The creative minority within the proletariat is thoroughly convinced of this fact and hence is ready to rally the masses behind almost any leader who will promise them a higher status and more things.

On the other hand, while this upward-reaching group in the lower classes is intent on changing the status quo for themselves and their supporters by any and all means, the top classes are intent on preserving the social structure and the rewards it provides. In most countries the intensity of the conflict is directly proportionate to the degree of separation and the strength of the intervening barriers.

Techniques of mobility

Though we often speak as though political events were the dominant factors in the change of class membership, this is essentially a false assumption. A change of political parties may slightly modify the rules by which persons may change social status, e.g. giving preference to those of liberal or conservative orientation, as the case may be, but for the most part it takes a thoroughgoing revolution to break open the social structure. Even the Mexican Revolution, one of the most drastic in Latin American history, did not completely overturn the social structure. What it did accomplish was to remove some of the first-class elite and to remove the caste restrictions on the lowest classes. It ultimately had a profound effect on Mexican society, in that it released social pressures bent on upward mobility, but it was far from being a Communist-style revolution. In this kind of revolution the higher classes are liquidated or reduced to lower-class status, and the revolutionary leadership takes over the places of the elite and erects a high wall of isolation between the party leadership and all the rest of the classes. What is more, the Communist social structure functions so as to draw its leadership not from the immediately inferior middle class of professionals but from exceptional persons in the lower class, who are not likely to favor competition from the potentially "dangerous" professionals.

For a woman the surest means of raising one's status is to marry into a family with higher social rank, for the husband's social position is largely the determining factor in a wife's status. If a man marries "above himself," he may or may not make the grade. This will depend upon personal charm, money, and, in the case of the first-class elite, primarily the willingness of his father-in-law to give him social status.

In many segments of Latin society the parents' obtaining for their children a *compadre* "godfather" or *comadre* "godmother" of a higher status than themselves is a means of going up in social rank. This is only a kind of indirect benefit, but it does serve to enhance the prestige and tie the social unit together.

Obtaining a *padrino* is another important method of advancing in social standing. A *padrino* is a person who agrees to help his "client" in business, often guarantees loans, protects him against abuse by other elite, seeks opportunities for his advancement, and introduces him to a higher social group than the person enjoys at the time. In return the "client" always supports the *padrino's* ambitions. If the *padrino* should ever have need, the "client" is supposed to help to the limits of his resources. This is, of course, a carry-over from feudal times, but it is a very important contemporary feature of Latin American life, and though it exists on a strictly informal basis (that is to say, there are no legal contracts binding the two parties), as a social institution it lies at the very heart of Latin life.

A number of other techniques in upward mobility have already been mentioned in other connections, namely, the acquisition of wealth, distinction in artistic performance, brilliance of intellectual endowments, and unusual leadership ability.

Orientation of the Roman Catholic Church toward Latin American society

In view of the fact that the Roman Catholic Church has been traditionally an authoritarian institution with a pyramidal structure, it has understandably concentrated its attention on the cultivation of the elite. Not only are all the major benefits of the Roman Church open to such people, but the Roman Church has generally obtained its leadership, from bishops on up, from the elite. In turn, the Church has provided the elite with the best possible education in the Roman Catholic tradition. Whether the masses remained illiterate or not has not always been a primary concern. In the past, what has counted has been the identification of the interests and viewpoints of the ruling group with those of the Church.

On the other hand, Protestants have generally directed their appeal to the masses, not only because they were more numerous, but because they were more concerned with change and responded to the hope of a better chance.

The Protestant appeal to the masses has seemed to many Roman Catholics as being nothing but a veiled form of Communism, since Communist agents likewise appeal to the lower classes and hold out promises of a better life. Protestantism and Communism have seemed sufficiently similar to convince the less informed or the already prejudiced that they must "repudiate the Communist and Protestant propaganda," as Roman Catholic publicists have repeatedly declared.

Justification of the Protestant approach

Some persons have questioned whether Protestant missionaries did right in appealing primarily to the lower classes. Certain individuals have contended that a concentrated "attack" on the leadership of Latin America would have ultimately resulted in greater gains. However, it is extremely doubtful that this would have been the case, even if the personnel capable of such an appeal to the upper classes had been available. All that one can judge from the results of Protestant work, in the light of the structure of Latin society, seems to confirm the view that early missionaries acted in accordance with sound sociological principles, even though at the time they did not analyze the problems or define the goals in these terms.

The sociological principles which seem to justify the course of most Protestant missions in Latin America are three:

1. The future always rests with the masses. This is particularly true in contemporary society, in which the vestiges of feudalism are rapidly crumbling in the assault of the so-called "mass man."

2. The creative minority (to use Toynbee's phrase) which is reshaping Latin life has its origin primarily in the upper-lower class and the lower-middle class, the very groups to which Protestantism directed its approach.

3. The only way to "raise" the masses is to become identified with them. The biblical principle of the leaven in the lump seems to be the only means of altering in any substantial way the condition of the masses. Even if the elite were won to Protestantism, there would be no guarantee that these persons, whose social position depends upon preserving the

status quo, would feel any constraint to change the condition of the lower classes, except in some superficial manner of urging a change of ecclesiastical loyalty on the part of the lower-class "subjects."

Despite what seems to be an evident sociological justification for Protestant strategy, one must also ask whether there has been a corresponding theological basis, or has the historic approach been essentially opportunistic? The answer to this question seems to be quite clear. There is a theological justification, for in essence this approach to the masses reflects the divine principle underlying the incarnation, namely, (1) humbling of oneself in order to identify and (2) giving leadership to others by participation and the challenge to "follow me." However, in many instances Protestants have given lip service to such principles, rather than practicing them "with a whole heart."

Though for many years the Roman Catholic clergy in general was relatively unconcerned with the condition of the lower classes, within the last few decades the social consciousness of Roman Catholic leaders has changed radically. Though some of the traditionalists continue to identify themselves and the interests of the Church with the elite, the younger clergy have increasingly identified themselves fully with the masses in their plight. This new social conscience is especially conspicuous in Brazil, where a number of priests have been arrested for their revolutionary support of the poor.

The face-to-face and the urban societies

In working out the implications of identification with the masses, one encounters wide differences of practice and response in small face-to-face communities and in large urban agglomerations. What works in an urban situation often fails miserably in a small town, and conversely what appeals to rural people falls on deaf ears when directed to an urban audience. What, then, are the basic differences in the social structures and the most effective means of communicating to these diverse constituencies?

A face-to-face society is just what it implies, one in which all the members are known to one another and everybody knows all about everyone else. What is more, in such a group most people are related, either through blood or marriage, and if not in this way, then through the god-parents and *padrino* systems. Such a face-to-face society functions in many ways like an extended family and as such tends (1) to make collective decisions, (2) to have consid-erable inner cohesion, (3) to present a unified front against intrusion, (4) to be conservative in orientation, and (5) to be centralized in its control, within the structure of the family.

If, in approaching one of these face-to-face communities, it is possible to win over the leadership, one can soon gain access to the entire group. That is to say, the community follows the lead of the "ruling" family or group of elders, even as members of a family tend to follow the direction of the father, or other strong personality. On the other hand, if one succeeds only in isolating some of the disgruntled members of such a community and in making them the "leaders" of a newly formed church, it is very likely that one will never be able to penetrate very deeply into the community structure. Such a "church" will always be a kind of appendage to the social structure, isolated from its essential life and a haven only for the community outcasts.

Many people have thought that the best approach to a face-to-face society is to preach the Good News to the entire group and to challenge the community to accept the gospel as a group. This procedure does not overlook the necessity of in-dividuals making personal commitments, but it proceeds on the basis that a group accustomed to making group decisions should be confronted as a social unit. Some German mission-aries have been singularly successful in this approach in some of the face-to-face communities in Indonesia. Dr. Al-cibiades Iglesias, who carried on a remarkable work among his own San Blas people in Panama, adopted a somewhat similar approach. He did not isolate the Christians or him-self from the community but related the message of the gospel to the entire life of the community. A very similar approach was employed by the Baptists of the eastern part of Cuba, who sought to minister to all the needs of an entire community and make the gospel relevant to all without attempting to isolate or estrange individuals within the community life. Similar programs of evangelism have been undertaken more recently by various Roman Catholic missionary groups.

On the other hand, one must recognize that in Latin America the likelihood of an entire community's accepting the gospel as a unit is not very great. This means that any such church or group will be made up of people who are more likely than not to be a minority in a community. As a minority they will be subjected to all kinds of severe social pressures, depending largely on (1) the extent to which the group is composed of those who are already regarded as community outcasts (hence the importance of not formally organizing a church until it contains at least some of the responsible members of the community, who are not subject to the same patterns of rejection) and (2) the degree of pressure which the traditional clergy can arouse concerning this "intrusion" into the community life.

Compensation for social pressures

When social pressures are brought against a newly established church, there must be some types of compensation or the entire church structure is likely to collapse. These people need to experience a kind of fellowship which is even more satisfying than what they have known in the community as a whole. If people can be taught the meaning of their new fellowship in Christ Jesus and what the "new community of the saints" can and should mean, they can be brought into a type of fellowship which will be not only satisfying but creative. The difficulty is that too often this in-group feeling is largely defensive, rather than creative; and though it does protect the members, it is largely ineffective in reaching out for others.

One of the very important ways of compensating for the loss of a feeling of social security within the immediate face-to-face community is to relate the small Christian community to a larger fellowship of other believers in the country. This is done by attendance at rallies, conventions, and official meetings of various church associations, so that they may realize that they are a part of a large, growing body of believers. In Peru one missionary discovered that it was of immense importance to have such meetings in towns which had newly established churches. If the small, struggling church could be the host to a relatively large group of people, who by their dress and behavior exhibited obviously higher social status than was regularly attributed to such groups, the impact upon the community would be of great importance in the evangelistic efforts of the church in question.

The approach to the urban community is by no means as restricted as that involving the face-to-face society. The urban community is made up largely of people who are dislocated from their former face-to-face communities. They are more independent, more easily attracted into new movements, and more anxious to find means of personal profit and advancement. In the largely impersonal atmosphere of the city, where one fights with one's neighbors but does not know them, the church has a very special ministry, for it can help to create an effective, mutually beneficial social group in the midst of the impersonal environment and thus meet people's basic need for fellowship. This aspect of personal fellowship in the midst of an impersonal society is one of the keys to the unusual success of the Pentecostal churches in Latin America. In addition to possessing a number of other extremely significant appeals to Latin temperament and values, these churches have succeeded in large measure in making people of all classes, and especially the very lowest, feel that they belong, are needed, and must make their own distinctive contribution within the community of believers which recognizes them as an integral part. This sense of belonging, of social security, and of being "indispensable" has resulted in the Pentecostal group's far outdistancing so many of the denominations which have depended more on trained leadership, foreign funds, and an emphasis on what the church could do for the people rather than what the people must do for the church. In other words, the Pentecostal churches have succeeded in large measure in creating a face-to-face, living fellowship in the midst of a competing, impersonal agglomeration of people.

Problems of a divided society

Within a face-to-face society, there may be an almost insuperable barrier which excludes one group from any vital social contacts with the other. In Latin America this situation exists in those communities which contain both Indians and

Latins. Except for some of the strictly primitive groups (as in Amazonia and a few other marginal areas), the Indians of Latin America are a part of the larger social unit. The culture is basically a folk culture, and the Indians stand in a dependency relationship. The whites are dependent on the Indians for some simple artifacts and for work and raw products from their small farms. The Indians are dependent on the whites for legal rights, guarantee and possession of their farms, rudimentary education, and all sorts of manufactured articles. There is a kind of symbiosis, with the white community being largely parasitic on the labors of the Indians.

This type of arrangement, involving dependency and exploitation, almost inevitably produces severe strains of feeling, deep suspicion, and outright antagonism. One would think that in view of this situation Protestant missionaries could make a strong appeal to Indians to "throw off the shackles" and to separate themselves from the religious system identified with the upper class. However, this is not easy, for the Indians know full well that their economic and social security depends very largely upon their maintaining a good relationship with the *patroncitos* "landlords and sponsors" or *palancas* "levers," as they are called in Ecuador. Some missions have attempted to minister exclusively to Indians and peons and have discovered that unless they actually controlled the land, as in the case of the Canadian Baptist mission in Guatajata, Bolivia, they had little or no success. In fact, some of the people whom they helped the most seemed most intent on proving their continued identity with the upper class by spending large sums of money on liquor with which to entertain the *patroncitos*. Wherever missions have experienced any appreciable success in working in such divided societies, it has been found that in some measure they either fulfilled the role of *patrón* or that there were some persons in the Latin society who would act as *padrinos* for the new believers.

Means of communication

Without doubt, one of the most difficult aspects of evangelism in Latin America is to discover those means by which the communication of the gospel may be made in a relevant and socially acceptable manner. This does not mean that the Good News must be distorted in order to accommodate it to men's ideas. Rather, it must be presented in such a context as to make it really "Good News," not just strange propaganda.

One Protestant missionary working in an Indian community of Ecuador discovered that the people were not at all interested in the beliefs of the Protestants, but they were very anxious to know about Catholic doctrines. Accordingly, in response to their requests, he agreed to tell them about the various Roman Catholic beliefs, and in a series of evening meetings in his own home he explained to them, without attempting to criticize or argue, the various doctrines of the Roman Church. He used a Roman Catholic catechism and employed a Roman Catholic copy of the Scriptures. After several evenings of teaching and discussion, some of the group insisted that he tell them what the Protestants believed. He then explained, in the same objective and meaningful way, what he as a Protestant believed. In the very community where other missionaries had been singularly unsuccessful in presenting the gospel, this missionary was able to communicate effectively because he spoke to the people's need and in a context relevant to their understanding at the time.

A missionary in West Africa made it a regular practice in his earlier days of itinerant evangelism to stop in villages for several days and in the evenings to inquire of the elders as to their belief in God. He never tried to explain his own faith until asked to do so by the elders, who invariably inquired of him after he had spent long hours in learning from them. The missionary's purpose was not, however, just to elicit curiosity. He was convinced that in order to tell the people about God he had first to learn what they knew about God, or otherwise he might fail utterly to make his message relevant.

One outstanding missionary in Peru has made it a practice never to enter a village to evangelize the people except at the express invitation of some person within the village. His Quechua helpers often enter new villages in order to establish important first contacts, but the missionary became convinced that if he was not to thwart the ultimate effectiveness of his ministry, he had to enter a village as a guest of

50818

a member of the community, who would not only guarantee his safety during his stay but would be an important means of inviting others to hear the Good News brought by the "foreigner."

There is a considerable tendency for missionaries to "barge ahead" irrespective of the local situation. One way in which this is done is through the free distribution of Scriptures and other Christian literature. Such materials seem to be so inexpensive and people appear to be so ready to accept whatever is offered free that missionaries are deceived as to the ultimate effectiveness of their endeavors. In the first place, a high percentage of such literature is never read, and not infrequently the people react against the gospel as being nothing more than cheap propaganda. In the process of selling, whether or not the person buys, the bookseller has the chance of witnessing to the truth and effectiveness of the Good News. He also has a chance to challenge the prospective customer to study this for himself and to accept it. However, the man who is distributing free literature is immediately classed as a propagandist, a job for which it is assumed he must be well paid. Accordingly, his own testimony becomes relatively valueless.

The necessity of communicating within a meaningful context may sometimes lead to amazing methods. One agriculturalist working with the YMCA in Mexico discovered that in the area in which he had set out to help the people everyone was suspicious of his efforts and refused to listen to his advice. Accordingly, the agriculturalist proceeded to introduce improved varieties of vegetables, grains, and fruits and employed new methods of putting humus back into the soil by the generous use of compost made from abundant organic material in the area. So the villagers would not "misinterpret" his efforts, he put up a high fence around his gardens and ostensibly attempted to protect his choice products. The inevitable result was that the people stole his produce to get seeds and cuttings; and to cultivate the plants they carefully imitated his methods. This method of teaching might seem unnecessarily "indirect," but it was effective, since it was fully meaningful within the context of these people's lives.

The importance of communicating by identification has been so emphasized that some missionaries have wrongly

Lincoln Christian College

exaggerated its significance to the point of thinking that identification consists primarily in imitation, largely of an external type. This has led some missionaries purposely to dress poorly and to live in ostensibly humble quarters. The people, however, have usually detected the false ring in this type of superficial imitation and have reckoned it as a kind of cheap paternalism, which in fact it is. The identification which is required is not imitation but full participation as a member of the society. In order to participate effectively one must not deny his own cultural heritage— something which cannot be done even if one wished to do so— but to employ this background for the benefit of the total constituency.

Some persons have insisted that "natives can best reach natives" (as they have so often framed the principle). In a sense this is quite true, but converts often refuse to work among people of the very class from which they themselves have come or among those who are in the immediate class below them, especially if these classes are both rather low on the social scale. This should not be too hard to understand, for any person who has advanced in the social structure as the result of hard work and diligent application often feels quite insecure in his new social position. To return immediately to work among people representing the very class from which he has raised himself would seem to endanger his status. Furthermore, a great deal of the education which he probably has received has prepared him for a middle-class social position, and in a sense he has been "declassified" as far as his original status was concerned. He no longer really feels at home. But even those who have not been educated up and out of a class are often reluctant to minister to people immediately beneath them. It would seem to imply that they are lowering their own status and hence endangering their prestige position within the society. On the other hand, such persons are often quite willing to work among those considerably below their own status, since then they do not feel that there is any danger of being mistaken for a member of such an inferior class. In a sense this explains why it is somewhat easier to get missionaries from the United States to work in areas in which nationals of the respective countries are reluctant to serve. The missionary runs no

risk of losing status. In fact, among the in-group of which
he is a part in the United States his very going to such
"benighted heathen" enhances his prestige, but this is not
the case with so-called national workers.

The sensitivity of national workers to the problems of
class within their own society must be fully recognized
if one is to understand their special problems and some of
the reasons which dictate what appears to be strange
behavior. In one instance, for example, an Indian from
southern Mexico went off to study in a Bible school in
Guatemala. Upon his return he began preaching in Spanish,
which he did with considerable skill, but of course his
audience understood little if anything of what he was saying.
This went on for about three weeks, after which the young
Indian pastor shifted to the Indian language and continued
to use it thereafter. Ability to use Spanish was an essential
symbol of his new status, and once this was adequately
confirmed, he could then safely afford to identify himself
with the Indian constituency.

This principle of security in social position helps to
explain why it is sometimes easier to get university
students to undertake work in some slum area than to get
people who have just emerged from the slums to return to
them in order to minister. This also explains why one
Negro pastor in Cuba found it difficult to work among his
own people; they preferred to have a white minister, since
this gave their church more prestige. On the other hand,
a well-educated constituency of whites was quite willing to
accept this brilliant Negro, since the prestige of this group
would not be endangered.

Backsliding and class identification

One of the apparently puzzling phenomena in the experience of some evident converts is the almost pathetic
concern for reinstatement which characterizes those who go
back into their former socioreligious grouping. Time and
again missionaries have mentioned how incredible it was
that certain people who seemed to show every promise of
developing into outstanding leaders would go "so far back
into sin," once they dissociated themselves from the
Evangelical constituency. In fact, such persons often

become far more addicted to their favorite vices than they ever were before coming in contact with the gospel. It would seem that the more conspicuous had been their testimony the more severe was their backsliding. The sociological explanation for this is the fact that such persons feel constrained to do all they can to be accepted again in the constituency of which they were formerly a part. To do this they must completely violate the mores associated with the group they have left in order to prove to their non-Protestant friends that they no longer belong to the Protestant group. A somewhat similar reaction occurs, of course, with the new convert to Protestantism. In order to be accepted in the Evangelical community, he often thinks he must symbolize his break with the past by strong denunciation of his former friends, publicized destruction of his images, and harsh criticism of the Roman Church, even to the point of quite unwarranted disrespect for the sentiments of conscientious people.

The work of the Holy Spirit

From what has been said up to this point, some readers might conclude that there is practically no role for the Holy Spirit in the program of evangelism. Quite to the contrary, the more one studies the methods and procedures of evangelism, the more one becomes convinced of the function of the Spirit of God in transforming the lives of people. However, it does seem quite evident that God's Spirit works with and not contrary to the basic need of human beings, as exemplified in certain aspects of social structure. A study of the human elements in the divine-human drama of God's role in human history does not deny God's part; it only helps one to appreciate better the way God has chosen to work within the context of human life by the principle of incarnation, rather than from outside by a continued series of supernatural interventions.

Those who fully appreciate the living reality of the incarnational element in our Christian faith take seriously the meaning of revelation by word and by life ("the Word became flesh"). On the basis of this the fundamental procedure of true evengelism may be developed in terms of identification ("He humbled himself") and participation

("He was tempted in all points"). Herein lies the key to effective witness, sacrificial ministry, and vital growth for the cause of Christ in Latin America.

6
Christo-Paganism[1]

Part of the difficulty foreigners have had in understanding Christo-paganism as practiced by many Indian groups in Latin America stems from the fact that they have not realized the basis for its complexity.[2] They are confronted with what is neither pure "animism" (or "primitivism") nor classic Roman Catholic beliefs and practices. Rather, there are subtle combinations of beliefs, often viewed by outsiders merely as a series of incredible superstitions containing self-evident contradictions. In many areas the system seems more strongly entrenched than ever, more firmly rooted in the soil of village life. Christo-paganism has different manifestations in different areas, for the indigenous ingredients which have entered into it are different, depending upon the local practices of the diverse tribes. Even when the pre-Columbian practices were similar, the resulting mixtures with the Roman Catholic system were often quite distinct. Furthermore, these mixtures have appeared on at least three different levels of religious syncretism.

On one level there is the almost purely indigenous religious system preserved by the *brujo* "sorcerer" and the *curandero* "medicine man," with only a superficial addition of Spanish holy words, incantations, and Catholic images. At the other extreme there is the typical church-centered

worship of the town-dwelling and Spanish-speaking Roman
Catholic, whose beliefs and practices are quite orthodox
except for a scattering of Indian magic and beliefs about
native herbs and medicines and possibly about some evil
spirits in a distant cave. Between these two extremes
there are varying degrees of Christo-paganism, a kind of
two-headed system which has two distinct, but noncontradic-
tory, orientations. On the one hand, the person looks to the
God of heaven, the priest, and the Church, and in this he
is quite a good Roman Catholic. On the other hand, he also
looks to *Dios Mundo* "the God of the World" (owner of the
mountains, valleys, rivers, and springs), the sorcerer,
and the *ermita* "local shrine."

The two-headed system is not only the possession of
people who speak some Indian language. In some regions
people no longer speak any indigenous tongue and yet they
continue to have a religious life which is a complex amalgam
of two theoretically disparate systems. To those who participate in syncretistic religion, there is no essential incom-
patibility between the different beliefs. Of course, there are
contrasts between related beliefs and quite diverse blends
of belief, but fundamentally the Indian appears to have what
is for him a not inconsistent set of concepts about the
world in which he lives and the spirit forces with which
he must deal. In fact, out of two systems, which from the
biblically oriented background should be in direct conflict,
he has created a quite consistent view of the world, himself,
and the supernatural, since he has found basic similarities
which outsiders have perhaps not noticed and he has reacted
quite sensibly to the obvious implications of the religious
teachings to which he has been exposed.

If we are to understand this "restructured" system,
we must take a close look at the underlying concepts about
the spirit world and how the individual behaves toward such
a world. It is possible to understand this restructuring only
if we attempt to see it as the Indian sees it.

The spirit world

For the typical Guatemalan Indian, for example, the
supernatural world is pluralistic, filled with a variety of
spirit powers, starting with *Dios Mundo* "the God of the

world," who is *dueño* "owner" of the entire earth and all that
is in it, and going on down to the *aires* "winds," which
seem to be the most impersonal, inimicable spirit forces,
causing all sorts of ailments. There are also the *nahual*,
a kind of forest sprite, and animals which are really spirits
in disguise. Moreover, there are all kinds of spirits which
are spoken of as *dueños* "owners," for these are the
responsible spirit possessors of such geographical features
as the mountains, valleys, streams, rivers, caves, springs,
canyons, and waterfalls.

In fact, almost every significant object of nature has a
spirit owner which must be properly propitiated if his
"property" is to be exploited. That is to say, before the
corn is planted, the *dueño* of the hillside must be prayed to,
or in anger he will ruin the crop, bring sickness to the
farmer, or withhold the rain. There is, of course, the sun
god, who created the world, and the moon, which is
responsible for the nurture of the crops. But these heavenly
deities do not figure so much in the indigenous system as
does *Dios Mundo*, who is a strictly autochthonous deity.
The creator god of the sun is supposed to have gone off
and left his creation, and the moon is not such a force as
the *dueño* of the soil, the god of earth.

In contrast with this system, the Roman Catholic set
of beliefs should be quite the opposite, since Christianity
is formally monotheistic. As a matter of fact, however, the
type of Christianity which came to these Indians of Guatemala
was not monotheistic. Nor was it dualistic, in the sense of
a conflict between God and Satan, each with an array of
heavenly emissaries in the form of good and bad angels.
Rather, from the Indian standpoint Roman Catholicism
presented an essentially polytheistic system, for *Dios* "God"
was spoken of as "God of heaven" and thus quite readily
equated with the sun. Moreover, he was quite removed
from his creation. It would seem that he had turned over
most of the day-to-day "religious work" to the saints,
who could be readily equated with the *dueños*. The bad
spirits were readily equated with the Christian demons, the
Virgin became the moon, the symbol of benefits and fertility,
and the offspring of God and the Virgin was Jesus Christ,
the symbol of death and dying. This was quite parallel to
certain indigenous pre-Columbian beliefs in which the god of

the dead was depicted as the son of the sun and the moon.

Faced with the two systems, indigenous and Roman Catholic (as presented in that day), the Indians had very little difficulty in restructuring the slight discrepancies into a single intelligible whole. They were already very much preoccupied with death, as is so well documented by the contents of the *Popol Vuj*, which recounts the religious legends of the Quiches as written down a few years after the conquest. Jesus Christ, as the symbol of death, becomes the god of the lower world and the judge of the dead, while the Virgin, his mother, continues to grant benefits to mankind and to intercede with the god of the dead. *Dios Mundo* becomes a kind of glorified Satan, because he is basically unpredictable and cruel. Moreover, even in Christian theology Satan is described as "the prince of this world," and hence there is a place for *Dios Mundo* in the Roman Catholic system. The saints, since they are readily attached to persons (who are named after them) and to prominent geographical objects, shrines, and churches, become the local *dueños*, who must be appeased and propitiated in order to insure the harmonious continuance of the processes of nature.

Since God was too far off to be much concerned (even though in the sun he might be trying to spy on us), the fact that he left the management of the world to the saints meant that the focus of attention was the saint, who could be visually represented in an attractive image. It was this image which simply took the place of the pre-Columbian idol. In some instances the old idol was merely given a Christian name. This shift from stone objects to those of wood and plaster-of-paris was quite bluntly explained to some tourists by a Roman Catholic taxi driver in Mexico City. He said, "What the Church did was to break the ugly stone images and give us pretty wooden ones."

The control of supernatural forces

The objectives of the indigenous and Roman Catholic systems were somewhat different. The Indian religion sought to maintain harmony with an unpredictable and essentially adverse universe, and the Roman Catholic religion proposed a method whereby man might overcome his fate through supplication to God and the saints. The fundamental techniques for gaining the desired ends, however, were essentially similar, since both were based on a bargaining relationship. It was the old Latin formula of *do ut des* "I give in order for you to give" (or "I'll help you if you help me"). These bargaining ends were to be accomplished by vows, sacrifices, gifts, penance, etc. —techniques which were quite similar in the two systems.

Basically, the techniques of control were designed to prevent difficulty, to correct trouble, and to cause harm. In each of these areas there were many common features. All of these techniques were lumped together under the heading of *costumbres* "customs," a Spanish word with a wide meaning, since it includes all traditional patterns of behavior, and yet with a narrow meaning, in that it specifically implies those particular types of behavior which have heavy religious significance. Since the people made no such distinction as we often make between the "secular" and the "sacred," this specifically religious connotation of the word was by no means contradictory or out of place.

Preventive religious practices

Since the indigenous concern for maintaining proper relations with the supernatural powers was a dominant theme in the religious life of the people, it is no wonder that the preventive rites, which included rituals of planting and harvesting, sacrifices for rain and for the consecration of homes and buildings, and divination by means of such objects as crystals, beans, animal bones, and grains of corn were all highly important events. The use of fire and the burning of *copal* as an incense were deeply ingrained features of indigenous worship.

In Roman Catholicism there was another set of religious practices, fiestas for the saints, candles to be burned in front of the images, incense in the churches, the ritual sacrifice of the mass, and the elaborate pageants of Christmas, Easter, and carnival. The people were very much accustomed to spectacular religious dramatizations, for the ritualism of dance and acting has probably never been more highly elaborated than in the indigenous religious performances of Mexico and Guatemala. Moreover, adopting the religious ritual of a conquering power was taken for granted. This was already an established practice among the Indians themselves.

It was therefore not difficult for Indians to blend the old with the new. Soon they were sending their prayers to the sky by means of skyrockets and getting drunk to help Jesus Christ on the cross so that vicariously he would not experience pain any more than they did in their inebriate state. These Christian fiestas became essential rites for maintaining proper relations with the universe. It is for this reason that even today when some Evangelicals refuse to participate in fiestas they are often denounced as bringing on dire calamity. The people are certain that drought, pestilence, persistent rain, and epidemics can only have their cause in the pernicious behavior of those heretical individuals who are spoiling the delicate balance of nature. This means that there is no place in the indigenous society for the social dissenter. The life of the entire community depends on the participation of the entire community. Otherwise, the malignant forces of nature will harm the whole society.

Corrective religious practices

If preventive indigenous practices were not enough to avert trouble, other practices were guaranteed to restore health and bring back prosperity. On a personal level the medicine man would heal by means of herbs and prayers, often after having obtained a confession of some social sin. If necessary, he would bring back the spirit of a man which had gone out of him in a dream, or had fled from him when he fell out of a tree, or had been frightened away by the sight of some apparition. A specialist might also be called in to perform sacrifices for rain or to stop a tropical storm.

In Roman Catholicism also there were corrective religious practices: confession, incense in the church, and candles burned before saints. In a case of great calamity, a saint would be carried up and down through the town to ward off pestilence or to protect the people against their enemies. For the Indians, there was very little difference between burning incense in the church and copal at some mountain shrine. Gifts of feathers and sticks to symbolize one's prayers to the dueño of a cave were really not very different

from candles burned in front of a saint in order to remind
the saint of a request. Furthermore, the leader of the
local shrine was almost exactly the counterpart of the priest
in the city church. The only difference was that the Roman
Catholic priest was a professional (he remained a priest all
of his life), while the leader of the shrine served his various
religious functions in a set system of graduated activities,
finally to retire with honor.

Malevolent religious practices

For most indigenous peoples supernatural powers are
fundamentally amoral. That is to say, they can be used for
either good or bad. Hence, the sorcerer can use the power
of the mountain spirit to curse a man, particularly if he can
get a lock of his hair, a paring of a fingernail, or some
leftover food. Through sacrifices to evil spirits he can initi-
ate such harmful influences that only another more powerful
sorcerer can prevent from occurring.

Officially Roman Catholicism did not introduce sorcery,
but most 16th-century Spanish settlers, including the priests,
believed in black magic, and many people practiced it. Moreover, they employed methods very similar to those the
Indians used, even to trying to get some scrap of hair,
clothing, or dirt which belonged to the intended victim.
Then by means of effigies, burning, and imprecatory formulas, they endeavored to curse their enemies. This they were
convinced they could do, especially if they could recite the
Lord's Prayer backwards. It is not strange, therefore,
that sorcerers began to use the powerful religious names of
God, Jesus Christ, the Virgin, and the saints. By mixing
them with the names of the traditional deities of the earth,
they fashioned even more powerful curses. Moreover, since
the Spaniards themselves had great faith in the curses of
these sorcerers, and often employed them to cast spells on
other whites, the result was the rapid blending of the two
systems into one.

Ethical behavior

A religion cannot be analyzed purely in terms of its
ritual forms or its underlying beliefs. It must also be studied

from the standpoint of the so-called norms of ethical behavior, especially as these are related to the religious system. That is to say, one must ascertain whether and to what extent the gods, spirits, or supernatural powers enforce, prescribe, condemn, or punish certain types of conduct. The problem is twofold in that there are both negative and positive aspects. First, one must analyze those actions which are prohibited, and second, one must study those types of behavior which are encouraged and specifically promoted by the religious system as positive benefits.

Sins, big and little

Although in biblical Christianity the real issue is not *sins* but *sin*, in most religions and in many nonbiblical forms of what passes for Christianity, the focus of attention is *sins*, big and little. In fact, the tendency to range sins as to their seriousness, whether mortal or venial, is almost a universal habit. It is in this tendency to classify negative (or prohibited) behavior that one discovers the most important clues as to the real ethical and religious character of any religious system.

In the indigenous systems in Guatemala it is difficult to say just what sin is the greatest, but surely one of the most important classes of sins consists in mistreating the processes of nature. This includes pulling up corn plants, plowing beans under (a real problem for the agricultural expert trying to teach the value of legumes as "green manure"), digging a well, cleaning out a spring, and leaving corn on the ground. In fact, the very act of planting a cornfield, in that it means cutting down the timber and digging into the soil, must be carefully conducted and fortified with prayers, in which the Indian explains to the *dueño* of the mountain that he does not want to dig deep into his back, but "just to scratch your shoulder blade a little." This basic concept of preserving the balance of nature is very deepseated and often explains the reluctance many Indians have in introducing radical changes.

Akin to this basic concept of preserving harmony with the supernatural powers is the related insistence upon keeping the religious festivals, at the time of weddings, births, funerals, and especially on All Saints' Day, when the autochthonous preoccupation with death reaches its yearly zenith.

Of course, adultery, murder, and stealing (except from a rich *ladino*, person of Spanish culture) are condemned, since they are contrary to the peace and well-being of the small face-to-face society. But almost equally despicable from the Indian point of view are inhospitality and gossip, which cause divisions and rifts in the social structure. In fact, a gossiping wife who brings accusations against her husband for adultery is often thought to be more at fault than the guilty husband. The adultery might have gone on undetected and without socially harmful consequences, if only the jealous wife had not shown ill will by gossiping about the affair.

Another type of behavior which is similarly condemned for its divisive effect upon the society is ostentatious living. Any Indian who tries to show off his wealth by dressing up like a *ladino* or who attempts to "shame" his neighbors by fixing up his home is often condemned for pride. In fact, it is of great significance that many of the indigenous legends center on this theme of social pride, in some senses considered the worst of all evils.

Within the indigenous system there are also little sins, *pecadillos* rather than *pecados*. These are fornication, lying (though it is generally regarded as better to lie than to molest or embarrass people by telling them the truth), not providing for one's family, and not paying back money. On this last issue it is of interest to note that frequently Indians are very scrupulous to pay back money loaned for medicines, since the medicine is not regarded as being fully efficacious if some deception is involved. At the same time an Indian who is very lax in paying back money may be very careful to take back tools which he has borrowed. This, of course, reflects the difference between the pre-Columbian standards of social responsibility with tools and the post-Columbian introduction of money, which was usually obtained from a *ladino* or foreigner. Hence, to rob the rich (who by implication is an enemy) is only a kind of primitive justice.

Certain types of behavior regarded by some outsiders as sins are simply not on either of these lists of big and little sins. They include drinking intoxicating beverages (except

insofar as drunkenness might prevent a person from taking
proper care of his family), polygamy, and improvidence.
A man is expected to be careful not to disrupt the course of
nature. However, he is not required to make the fullest use
of the resources nature has given him. In other words, the
gods will bring woe to him if he violates the laws of nature,
but they will never punish him for failing to use the gifts
they have provided.

In the traditional Roman Catholic system, there are also
big and little sins, and the biggest one by all counts is
heresy, which manifests itself on a practical level by disrespect for the images, failure to take part in the fiestas,
and neglect of the dead on All Saints' Day. These ritual
observances are in many ways parallel in form and purpose
to those of the indigenous religious system, in that both
systems are designed to prevent the judgment of the supernatural upon the people.

At the same time, adultery, stealing (especially if one
steals a great deal and from the poor), and murder are also
big sins, but lying, fornication, and fighting are usually
very small sins. In fact, fighting is often regarded as no sin
at all, especially if it is designed to remove a stain of dis-
honor caused by some real or imagined insult. From Spain
the exaggerated knightly honor of the Middle Ages, which was
accentuated by the extreme Arabic insistence on honor
revenge, was brought to the Americas and among the *ladino*
population has continued as a justification for many kinds of
violence.

There are two types of behavior which Protestants generally regard as major sins but which many Roman Catholics
in Latin America refuse to classify as such; these are having
mistresses and drinking. The Roman Church has traditionally excommunicated a man for divorce, but there has been
no such record of stringent denunciation of the practice of
having mistresses. Even the prostitutes are regarded not so
much as being sinners as being most unfortunate, and thus
under the protection of their patron saint María Magdalena,
whose image graces many brothels.

Good deeds

In the indigenous and Roman Catholic systems, there are
also various kinds of behavior which are particularly recom-

mended and religiously rewarded in the sense that the spirits or saints are pleased and one's chances with the gods or God are therefore improved. In the indigenous system several types of deeds are of high esteem. These include hospitality, including taking time to entertain strangers and friends, the owning of one's own land and the raising of one's own corn (this is almost a religious duty in some areas), respect for elders and those in authority, and the assuming of one's rightful responsibilities in the socioreligious system of officeholding, including paying for elaborate fiestas when it is one's turn.

In the Roman Catholic system certain similar types of behavior are also highly regarded. Among them are the giving of alms, caring for homeless people, implicit obedience to religious authorities, and, to a lesser extent, to civil authorities (religious authorities have normally had the preeminence in traditional Roman Catholicism); also important are assuming financial responsibility for religious fiestas and spending in proportion to one's income. In other words, a person who does not spend his money, even though it be for pure ostentation, is guilty of miserliness, and that is regarded as a grave sin.

A study of these two systems of behavior, negative and positive, reveals some very significant parallels. In the first place, much of the focus of attention is upon ritual observance. In certain branches of Protestantism, ritual is reduced to a minimum, and the focus is upon social behavior. The issue then is put in terms of not how well a person can pray but how much good he can do. But in the indigenous and Roman Catholic systems, the greatest sins have often been regarded as failure to carry out the required ritual.

In both systems, fornication has been regarded as a relatively minor sin, along with lying, while extramarital or premarital sexual activity is almost outside of the classification of sin. When pressed, most Indians and *ladinos* will admit that such sexual behavior is not good, but it does not carry strong emotional feelings of guilt or appear to be so heinous as to result in any strong social stigma. Drinking of alcoholic beverages is no sin at all; in fact, drunkenness figures as an important element in the ecstatic character of many religious fiestas. By getting drunk one does honor to the saint. It should also be noted that in both of these systems there are very important responsibilities to be carried out by the rich and the well-to-do, while for the most part the poor stand on the sidelines.

Almost precisely at those points where the indigenous and Roman Catholic systems have been parallel and reinforcing, the typical Protestant presentation of the gospel has been most at variance. The average Indian or *ladino* in a small town who has heard something of Protestantism, tends to think that Protestants have very strange ideas. One must not drink, fiestas are bad, the images are worthless dumb idols, and fornication, polygamy, and any and all kinds of sexual immorality are very, very bad. Of course, the local Protestant evangelist may not have been so openly negative in his presentation of the gospel, but probably all that has gotten through to the casual listener is this opposition to certain kinds of behavior, some of which he would scarcely regard as sin at all (for example, having a mistress or a second wife), while others he would insist on as being highly desirable (for example, sponsoring a drunken fiesta).

If the Indian only learned more about the Protestant "ethic," he would discover that at one point it had very much in common with his own, namely, the emphasis on the value of work. However, he would not be likely to understand the Protestant glorification of work as such, as being the true purpose of existence, for Indians work so that they can enjoy "nonwork" or leisure; they see nothing therapeutic about work itself.

When an Indian does become interested in the message of a Protestant evangelist and even joins the church, neither he not his *ladino* Evangelical neighbor is very likely to feel a compulsion to contribute to the church. In their experience only the rich are supposed to pay for the fiestas. And since the Protestant Church has no fiestas and makes no charges for the services of the pastor (in the form of fees for baptisms, weddings, burials), there is neither a pattern nor an incentive for giving.

Religious functionaries

Having compared certain aspects of the beliefs and behavior of the two closely related religious systems, we must

also examine briefly certain features of the parallel types
of religious functionaries which exist almost side by
side.

In the strictly indigenous system, there are the Indian
religious specialists who are generally called in for important fiestas to offer the prayers and recite the incantations.
These men may be called from quite a distance, and their
utterances may be entirely in the Indian language or mixed
with Spanish.

Beneath these specialists are the leaders of the shrines,
laymen who are elected from among the people of a village
or section of a town to officiate at and to take care of the
local shrine, which houses the patron saint of the immediate
region. They must change the saint's clothes, wash them,
provide flowers, keep the shrine clean, organize the appropriate fiestas, and carry the saint about on special occasions.
Some of these local religious functionaries can recite the
Apostles' Creed, the Lord's Prayer, and the Ave Maria,
but their main job is to carry out ritual in honor of the local
saint, which in pre-Columbian times was a stone idol but at
present is a very attractive wooden or plaster-of-paris
creation.

Beneath the leaders of the shrine are the medicine men,
individual specialists in healing, who usually use a combination of herbs and religious incantations to heal the sick,
ward off evil, bless cornfields, and drive away blight. The
sorcerers are a fourth class, consisting of people who
generally deny that they are sorcerers if directly questioned
but who are thought to be able to manipulate powerful supernatural forces, whether for good or for evil, but usually with
the purpose of doing evil.

In the Roman Catholic system there is a similar array
of bishops, priests, lay brothers, nuns, and catechists, each
with his respective area of control and activity. These two
systems interlock at the points of the ritual (both the Roman
Catholic priests and the indigenous leaders use many of the
same prayers) and the blessing of the *ermitas* (generally a
local group is very much concerned that the local saint be
blessed by the priest). In fact, if the people can afford the
priest's services, he may be asked to come and inaugurate
various local fiestas. But otherwise the two patterns of
religious expression continue along parallel lines.

Two systems or one?

Most people regard Christo-paganism as being two different systems, or a blend of the two. It is better, however, to think of this combined system as a two-headed object (reflecting the different basic sources) with a single body, for fundamentally the two parts fit together into one whole, at least as seen through Indian eyes.

Of course, the Roman Catholic system to which the Indians of Guatemala have been exposed is not the form accepted among all Roman Catholics. In fact, some of the Maryknoll Fathers working in Guatemala have been zealously trying to correct local abuses of Roman Catholic tradition, and some of them have even been driven away by Indians who violently objected to any interference with their time-honored adoration of the saints. It is even reported that the Indians in one town in Guatemala accused an American priest of being a Protestant in disguise because he dared to quote the Bible against some of the traditional idolatrous practices.

For the most part, however, the Indians of Guatemala were originally confronted with no such "purified" form of Roman Catholicism. Rather, it was a traditional medieval form which was quite close to the indigenous beliefs and practices. The Indians easily added the attractive fiestas in honor of the saints and were ready to act out the conflict of the Christians and the Moors (a historical drama in Spain, but in the New World only a morality play between the good and the bad, the victorious and the vanquished). No trouble was involved in adding to the already loaded pantheon a few more deities (the saints), or in giving new names to the old ones. The Virgin as the moon was no great problem, for already in medieval Europe (as carvings on some cathedrals show) the same identification had been made. If the saints seemed a little too likely to see evil around them, there was always the expedient of blindfolding the saint before committing the crime; and each year during the day that Jesus was supposed to be in the tomb, people enjoyed a time of complete license to sin, for "God was dead."

There was evidently little objection to the added religious functionaries of the church, for this was essentially a complementary institution which provided spiritual benefits (for those who could afford them or understand them) but which were not necessary, since the indigenous pattern remained intact.

While the focus of the indigenous religion was *Dios Mundo* and the center of the Roman Catholic worship was the Church, the two met completely in the veneration of images. Here was common ground, for the symbol of this faith was the image, and the ecstasy was found in intoxication.

The strength of Christo-paganism

Anyone who has lived among the Indian tribes of Guatemala or Mexico knows very well indeed that the dual system of Christo-paganism is no flimsy patchwork of transient beliefs but a stronghold of tribal resistance and a symbol of ethnic unity. The bases of its strength are numerous, but perhaps the following are the most significant.

1. The integration of the religious system with the daily life of the people. For the Indian his religion is no mere fiesta experience but one which accompanies him constantly. He arises to greet *Tata Dios* "Father God," who is the sun, crosses himself before the image of the saint, carries flowers to the shrine, invokes the spirits of the field before beginning to work, consults a medicine man for medicine for a sick child, and meets at night by the shrine to plan for the fiesta of the patron saint. Moreover, the entire system of godfathers and godmothers, which tends to bind the social structure together, is dependent upon common religious sentiment and ritual.

2. The full use of lay leadership. One of the acknowledged weaknesses of official Roman Catholicism in Latin America is the tendency for too great a dependence upon the ordained clergy, but in the dual Christo-paganism there is no such danger. The indigenous part of the system is almost entirely in the hands of elected lay leaders, who would carry on the worship of the saints for generations, even if all the priests were driven from the land.

3. The religion as a symbol of ethnic unity. The Indians of Mexico and Guatemala have been hard pressed by the dominant Spanish-speaking peoples, so that in order to maintain their own way of life at all they have had to become increasingly resistant to outside influences. This has made them a highly sensitive kind of "peasant society," jealous

of their own distinctiveness and insistent upon preserving their religious heritage as a means of enforcing their own solidarity. This characteristic makes them suspicious of foreigners and extremely hesitant to adopt new ideas or ways of life. As part of this identification of religious uniformity with tribal unity, they have naturally treated heresy or nonconformity with fanatical opposition. Such fanaticism is not merely a Roman Catholic intellectual response to the traditional position that "error has no rights," but emotional reaction to a threat to the very existence of the group itself. A heretic becomes a traitor, and the mere dissident is a potential source of all kinds of evil.

4. The emphasis on social maladjustment rather than on personal sins. The fact that the indigenous religion is so strongly against nonsocial conduct such as gossiping, causing people to lose face, disrespect for elders, disobedience to authority, and disloyalty to the patron saint, is a strong reinforcement of the social bonds which keep the system going. Such personal sins as drunkenness, lying, and sexual immorality are not regarded as particularly bad unless there are unfavorable social results. Individuals are thus allowed a good deal of personal indulgence, provided the whole community is not made to suffer. This means that the system is morally weak where it hurts the social structure the least, and hence the result is a strong socioreligious system.

The weaknesses of Christo-paganism

Christo-paganism is a strong socioreligious system, but in many respects it is a weak religious faith. Though it tends to bind men closely together, it fails in a number of significant aspects.

People are left in an unfriendly universe of overwhelming spirit powers. Even if the spirits are not malevolent (and many of them are), they are certainly incredibly capricious in their judgments, and God is too far removed to be much concerned. In fact, it is this very religious insecurity which tends to make men cling closer together in various social bonds. There is absolutely no concept of Paul's statement that "in all things God is working together for good with them who love him" (Romans 8.28). Even the best native medicines and the most powerful incantations are only weak tools with which to cope with the onslaught of essentially merciless spirits. By judicious religious behavior, one may expect to improve his fate, but never to meet with any real ultimate success.

The demands of the religion are out of proportion to the benefits derived. For the enormous investment in fiestas the people receive actually very little in return, except a sense of prestige for having been the benefactors. Even those who engage fully in the system are not infrequently found to complain severely of the disproportionate costs, and many who become Evangelicals later admit quite frankly that they were very much influenced by noting the education, medicines, sufficient food, and adequate shelter which other believers had begun to possess after giving up the old way of life.

The central theme is death rather than life. Religion which has as its central theme the event and significance of death can have a tremendous power over people, but it cannot release their fullest creative energies, since people cannot psychologically identify themselves continuously with symbols of death and remain mentally healthy. They must relate themselves to life if they are to live usefully and creatively.

The ethics of Christo-paganism do not meet the elemental standards of equity. Even though a man may have recourse to black magic to harm a prosperous neighbor, he knows full well that this is not right, since it contradicts the universal requirement of reciprocity within the in-group. Putting a blindfold on the saint is no real way to solve the problem of guilt, and stealing is stealing, even though one's victim may have plenty. When confronted with the moral demands of Jesus Christ, the Indian may have plenty of excuses for his conduct, but he recognizes that there is no real justification for his anti-social behavior.

Despite the evident weaknesses in Christo-paganism one must not expect such a system to collapse of its own dead weight, despite encroaching secularism and increasing anti-clericalism among many better educated Indians. Certainly the mere proclamation of taboos against smoking, dancing, drinking, and gambling is not going to seriously affect such a system.

There are two points of interesting contact (or parallel-ism) between the indigenous religious pattern and typical Protestantism. They are the high premiums placed on the value of work, in and of itself, and the virtue of the simple way of life (the lack of ostentation); but North American Protestant missionaries are generally poor persons to preach or to demonstrate either of these points of view. They seldom seem to the Indian people to be working (working, for the Indians, is digging in a cornfield), and even the simplest material possessions compatible with health place the average missionary in an entirely different socio-economic class. Accordingly, the basic "answers" seem to be primarily the "theological" ones, and in the ultimate analysis these are the only answers that really count. How-ever, any presentation of the truths of the Scriptures must be given with full awareness as to their relevance to the people and in complete recognition of their radical difference from the indigenous point of view.

The following themes, phrased as direct declarations of the pagan versus Christian way of life, would seem to be the most relevant.

1. The spirits of the mountains and the valleys may be powerful, but they are nothing in comparison with the Spirit of God, whom all people may have as their protector and helper if only they are willing to receive God's way of life.

2. It is true that Christ died and in this way he showed men how to die, but what is more important is that he is now alive and he has shown men how to live.

3. It is not strange for people to think that God would go off and forget them, since their many sins would justify God's doing just that; but in reality he did not leave people alone. Because of his great love for those whom he created, he actually sent his Son into the world to show them beyond the shadow of a doubt that he really loves them.

4. If people have trouble because of quarrels, fights, drunkenness, and jealousy, this is not strange. How can people be any better than the spirits whom they fear and worship? But God has shown people a better way. As His children through Jesus Christ, they ought to love one another.

5. All men want to be better than they are, but they find they do not have the moral strength to do the things

they want to do. God knows this, and he has told people that they can receive the power to be what they know he wants them to be.

6. When people become believers in the living God, as revealed in Jesus Christ, they are not deserted and left alone, even if their former friends despise them. They become a part of a new family of God and belong to all the other believers. The new believer must not think that he belongs to the mission or to the missionary, but to the congregation of faith.

It is, of course, impossible at this point to elaborate in detail the almost infinite variety of ways in which these dominant themes must be told and retold, but in each instance the message begins where the people are, recognizing the facts of their present circumstances, and unfolds a new and vital way of life. In the various areas where there has been a significant spiritual awakening among the Indian peoples, these have been the themes which have been emphasized, but in each instance the power of the message has been the constant, repeated, and full presentation of the life and ministry of Jesus Christ, since he is the real distinction between Christianity and paganism.

7
Mariology in Latin America[1]

For a number of years, and especially just prior to Vatican II, there was a marked increase of interest in Mariology within the Roman Catholic Church. This increased focus of attention upon Mary has found expression in the establishment of many shrines, wide publicity of reputed miracles, numerous books and articles on the significance of Mary for the modern world, and intense promotion of the Virgin of Fatima as the protectress of Christendom against Communism. The promulgation of the doctrine of the assumption of the Virgin augmented Mary's theological status, and the much discussed doctrine of Mary as coredemptrix with Jesus Christ gained considerable influence within certain circles of the Roman Church.

For the most part, this development in Mariology has been discussed by Protestants primarily in terms of the theological implications of the ever increasing centrality of Mary within the Roman system. In large measure, however, Protestants have failed to see this development in terms of the broader cultural implications. In order to understand and more fully appreciate what is happening within the Roman Church, one needs to view this extraordinary emphasis upon Mary in the light of the anthropological background involved.

Dying Christ and living Mary

In trying to understand the reasons for focusing attention upon Mary, some persons have claimed that this is an almost inevitable result of making Christ less and less attractive to the people. Rather than the victorious "culture hero" (if one may speak in purely anthropological terms), Christ is portrayed as the defeated, dying victim. Such a Christ produces feelings of pity and compassion, but he does not inspire confidence and hope. Christ on the cross reminds the sinner of his sins, but this does not make the average person want to identify himself with the suffering Savior.[2] Contemplation of the dying Christ does elicit strong emotional feelings, but they tend to drain one of nervous energy. Accordingly, they do not result in a feeling of well-being or confidence.

In contrast with the dying Christ, the radiantly beautiful Mary is the benevolent one who is always accessible and always giving. It is Mary who has compassion for the multitude, and it is the contemplation of this symbol which brings reassurance and a sense of hope and well-being. As the mediatrix between the worshiper and Christ, or God, she becomes the giver of life, the source of health, and the means of power. It is not strange, therefore, that for many persons the center of worship in the Roman Church has shifted from Christ to Mary. People prefer to identify themselves with a living Mary rather than with a dying Christ.

The mass and fertility rites

This contrast between death and life has been further accentuated in the Roman development of the mass, which in its early New Testament form reflected the covenant meal of the Old Testament. However, during the first few centuries it became in many aspects assimilated with the fertility cult rites of the mystic religions. Whether as reflecting the rites of Eleusis, Isis, or Osiris, or as reflecting those which centered in the cult of Astarte, the same dominant principle prevailed—the dying god-son raised to life through the principle of female productivity. As the mass developed, it became no longer a commemorative feast, but a miraculous reenactment of the shedding of blood. The worshiper

was reminded of the fact not just that Christ died and rose
again but that he was constantly dying for the people, and
they partook of his very body and blood, whether directly
or in the person of the priest. This symbol served only to
reinforce their equation of Christ with death and not with
life. The emotional unattractiveness of this procedure left
a spiritual and psychological void which was filled by the
symbol of the Virgin—readily borrowed from the pagan
mystery religions and taken over with very little adaptation
into the practices of the Church, though with a certain
measure of theological polishing.

The Latin American culture context

The fact that the symbol of the suffering, dying Christ
was gradually replaced by the loving, living Mary is, however, by no means all of the story, particularly in the case
of Latin America. There the developments have an even
deeper significance as far as their relationship to the cultural themes are concerned. In the Ibero-American culture
(excluding the Indian elements), the Church and the society
seem to fit like a glove on a hand, and quite understandably
so, for in a sense the glove and the hand "grew up together."
The Latin culture has been in a large measure the product
of the teaching of the Church, and in turn the Church has
adapted itself to special Latin characteristics. Any attempt
to discover the order of priority (the old problem of the
chicken and the egg) is a relatively fruitless undertaking,
since such adjustments always come as successive waves of
give and take. However, within the contemporary life of
Latin America certain important observations can be made
concerning the reciprocal reinforcement of the related
institutions, and it is this phase of the cultural pattern which
one should note.

Female orientation

There are three underlying factors which must be understood, if one is to appreciate the close relationship between
the Roman Church and Latin American society. In the first
place, Latin American culture is female-oriented. By this
we do not imply that this orientation is the only or even the

dominant one, but in contrast with some cultures which in this area of life may be described as sex-oriented, certainly Latin American culture shows a dominant tendency toward female orientation. In the society of the United States (as well as in the culture of ancient Greece), the dominant element seems to be more a matter of sex itself than of interest in the female. These differences may be noted in such Latin American characteristics as (1) machismo, (2) more overt attention paid to sex characteristics of females, and (3) greater concentration of interest in eliciting female response than in simply gratifying sexual drives. Furthermore, the greater distinctiveness in male and female roles tends to reinforce the female-oriented nature of Latin society.

The mother role

In the second place, in Latin American society the mother is the emotional center of the family. The father is more or less expected to have extramarital relations, whether with prostitutes or mistresses. In fact, in some regions of Latin America the number and quality of one's mistresses is a more decisive factor in gaining prestige than the number of cars one owns. Since the father is expected to have divided loyalties and to possess other emotional attachments, it is not difficult to understand why children should feel greater emotional attachment to their mother, even though they may continue to have a deep respect for their father. In saying that the father is expected to engage in extramarital affairs, we do not imply that all men do, for some are very faithful to their families, especially those in the middle and lower income groups. However, though some fathers may not be unfaithful, there is nevertheless the general attitude that if such men should become unfaithful, they are not to be too severely condemned. Furthermore, the wives in such circumstances are supposed to be more or less tolerant toward such affairs and to accept with equanimity the fact of competition.

A more or less natural consequence of the mother's role as bestower of benefits from the time the children are quite small is that she continues to function in this same way, though in a somewhat different form. Rather than being the direct source of help, she becomes the intercessor for the children with the less approachable father. In fact, fathers are supposed to be somewhat standoffish and mothers are supposed to be more indulgent. Of course, there are numerous exceptions to these roles, but this is the general pattern. Even though in a particular community this pattern may not be the statistically dominant one, it is, nevertheless, regarded by most Latins as being the way Latin life is organized. Hence, the "myth" (or the reality) of the more distant father and the interceding mother becomes a cultural framework in which the concept of an exacting God and a benevolent Mary can have meaning.

Women in the Church

In the third place, there is a very well-defined relationship of reinforcement between the status of women and the position of the Church. The status of the wife in an outwardly monogamist society is maintained by the Church by denying the validity of divorce. In fact, in some countries of Latin America the Roman Church has had such influence upon the governments that there is no possible way for a person to obtain a legal divorce. The Church, accordingly, confirms and maintains the wife's status by legally preventing or by placing severe obstacles in the way of any other female threatening the position of the wife. At the same time, the mores of the society permit almost wholesale competition for the romantic affection of the husband. But by threat of excommunication against divorcees (though not against mistresses or adulterers) status is maintained, even though there is often a wide discrepancy between real and ideal roles and behavior.

It is, accordingly, quite understandable that the wife and mother should be concerned with reinforcing the authority of an institution such as the Church which does so much to protect her status. As the faithful, interceding mother, she identifies herself with the Virgin and finds her confidence in the strength of the one institution which maintains her status and defends her role.

Since there is also a rather well-defined pattern of indulgence of mothers toward sons, it is not difficult to see how in this aspect as well the people assume that the most effective way of reaching the somewhat formidable Christ is through the indulgent, benevolent mother. Accordingly, not only do women find in Mary a cultural type with which they may identify themselves, but many men, whether consciously or unconsciously, tend to transfer their feelings of dependence upon their mother to worship of the Virgin Mother.

All this means that loyalty to the Virgin is the result, not primarily of instruction by the Church itself, but of a kind of unconscious reflex of the underlying emotional patterns in Latin life. This is perhaps the principal reason why the Roman Church continues to be so powerful, despite the strong liberal and intellectual movements in Latin America. Time and again, the Jesuits have been forced out of various countries, and in many areas there are strong anticlerical movements; but despite such anti-Church attitudes, there seems to be a continued devotion to the Virgin as an unconscious symbol of the life of the people. It is not without significance that for each of the countries or principal regions in Latin America there is some patron Virgin. Individual areas may also have their patron saints, but the overruling focus of emotional attachment is generally to the Virgin. This promotion of the Virgin as the patron of the nation is a natural outgrowth of the role of the benevolent mother.

Male-oriented cultures

In contrast with the centrality of Mary in Latin America, it is interesting to note the differences in the Greek Orthodox Church, as well as such other Eastern churches as the Coptic, Armenian, and Ethiopic. Though the Eastern as well as the Roman churches had a very similar early history as regards certain aspects of the mass and the recognition of Mary as "Mother of God" (a significant feature of the Athanasian and Arian controversy), nevertheless the Eastern Church has not made Mary the center of adoration to the extent that the Roman Church has done, especially in Ibero-American culture. Part of this disparity may be attributed to the fact that the Eastern Church rejected the use of images and sensuous art forms. Icons, relics, and mosaics were not particularly well adapted to emphasizing a female sex element. The Eastern churches are studded with frescoes

and murals, but these are predominantly of masculine
persons: biblical heroes, early saints, and Jesus Christ.
However, despite the difference in the art forms and
objects, one basic reason for this diversity between the
Eastern churches and the Roman ones is the fact that in the
area of the Eastern churches society is much less female-
centered. In this feature there has no doubt been some
influence from Islamic culture during the last thousand years
or so. But even before the rise of Islam, the culture of the
Eastern Mediterranean was essentially male-oriented.

Theology and emotions

The most frequent accusation leveled against Protestants
in Latin America is that they do not "believe in" the Virgin.
The accusation does not betray any special theological
concern for the Virgin; it is only that Latins cannot understand what seems to be a gross lack of respect, gratitude,
and filial loyalty. For the average Latin Roman Catholic
the Virgin is not primarily the historical personage who
lived in Nazareth, gave birth to Jesus Christ, and nurtured
him to manhood. Rather, the Virgin is the symbolic projection of a series of emotional attitudes formed within the
very first years of a child's life. Emotional attachment to the
Virgin is thus acquired as one of the deepest and earliest
psychological experiences. For the most part, this attitude
toward the Virgin is without overt reasoning, though it may
be formulated in memorized doctrines and expressed in
overt acts of prayer. The fact that Virgin adoration is
largely implicit within the cultural framework greatly
increases its strength for any rejection of the Virgin is tied
up with rejection of mother, home, and family love.

To a great extent, Protestant missionaries in Latin
America have failed to understand fully the place of the
"Virgin symbol" in the lives of Roman Catholics. They have
tried to employ theological arguments against what they
have denounced as "Mariolatry." However, for the most
part, Roman Catholics have been entirely unmoved by such
theological arguments. The reason for this is that they
learned to believe in the Virgin not from theological arguments but because of family relationships. Even though
they might admit the validity of arguments based on historical

revelations in the Scriptures, Roman Catholics find themselves emotionally unable to reject the Virgin. In fact, they
often insist that they know God would not want them to do so.
They have simply never distinguished between filial loyalty
and the religious symbol of the Virgin.

The living Christ

If, however, the break from the Virgin symbol is so
difficult for Roman Catholics, how is one to explain what has
happened for so many tens of thousands (at least five million
in all) who are Protestants in Latin America? There are,
of course, a number of more or less overt "anthropological"
reasons for people turning from Catholicism to Protestantism: (1) reaction to the authoritarianism of the Church,
(2) educational advantages offered by Protestant missions,
(3) personal resentment against the behavior of persons who
were identified with the Roman Church, and (4) a sense of
frustration which ends up in a nonconformist defiance of the
status quo and all it stands for. To this list may be added a
number of minor overt reasons why people become Protestants. However, there is another reason which is far more
important than any of these "trigger" causes. This is the
substitution of the symbol of the victorious, living Christ
for the defeated, dying one.

One of the effective ways in which this new symbol has
been communicated is through the Scriptures. Time after
time, traditionally oriented Roman Catholics have comment-
ed that until they read the Scriptures they "did not realize
that Christ lived." They had thought of him only as dying.
The fact that his life was filled so full of service and identification of himself with people and that, though he suffered,
he rose from the dead and ascended to glory, seems to be
an almost incomprehensible revelation.

Furthermore, in the message of the Scriptures Roman
Catholics discover that it was God who identified himself
with man in Christ (God is no longer screened off by the
ever-present Virgin) and that it was Christ who identified
himself wholly with man. It is this identification of Christ
with man ("he was one like us") which finally reaches
through to men and women. Furthermore, Roman Catholics
learn that this Christ who lived also lives today and by his

Spirit walks with men. Here is the fullness of fellowship and the certainty of penetrating through the veil which shrouds the well-meaning but sometimes thwarted efforts of the kindhearted Virgin symbol.

For the most part, Roman Catholics do not change their attitudes about the Virgin suddenly. In fact, during the process of learning about the living Christ, they often go back time and again to praying to the Virgin, and in times of severe family crisis they feel an almost irresistible urge to seek refuge in prayers and candles to the Virgin. When they do make a final break (sometimes after a number of years), they do so only when the symbol (and the reality) of the Christ as living intercessor has been completely substituted for the earlier symbol of the interceding Mother.

The symbol of the Lord Jesus Christ cannot hope to be as popular as that of the benevolent Mother, if by "popular" one means that which has the greatest appeal to the average person. In the first place, the Virgin symbol involves a physical attractiveness with sex appeal (whether admitted overtly or not—for who has ever seen an image of an ugly Virgin?) and an emotional identification with mother love. On the other hand, the symbol of the Lord Christ, though it may have some of the popular appeal of the culture hero, can never become simply a Davy Crockett. As God himself, Christ always possesses for man that "otherness" which mystified even his closest disciples. He was one with them, and yet they recognized that he was utterly different. This mystery of the incarnation never escaped them and continues both to mystify and to inspire the believer's deepest thoughts and his highest aspirations.

Celibacy of the priesthood

The celibacy of Roman Catholic priests would seem to rule out the sexual element in the Virgin symbol, but in reality it only confirms the sex factor. In his function as the earthly representative of Jesus Christ, the Pope and the priesthood which receive their sanction through him must be symbolically identified with Christ. However, in order to be intimately associated with the Virgin Mother symbol, they must be *symbolically* incapable of sex relations. Otherwise there would be danger of "spiritual incest." On the other

hand, the Protestant minister has no such attitudes toward
the Virgin symbol, and in his role of prophet, rather than
primarily of priest, he identifies himself with the people,
in order to proclaim to them the will of God. The Roman
priest, however, is primarily a priest, identified with the
bestower of benefits (i. e. the Virgin Mother) and transmitter
of blessings to the people.

The close relation between celibacy of the priesthood and
the Virgin symbol may be seen by comparing further the
practices of the Eastern and Roman churches. Asceticism
began in the East as the result, it would appear, of predominantly Syrian influences, in which celibacy of priests in
numerous pagan cults was regarded as an essential requisite
for attendance upon the goddesses of fertility. (In a number
of these religious cults, castration was the symbol of
identification with the goddess.) However, though celibacy
began in the Eastern churches and was widespread during
early centuries, it is not now regarded as a requisite for
the priesthood, even though it may be encouraged in some of
the orders and required for certain higher posts in the
ecclesiastical hierarchy. On the other hand, though celibacy
was relatively slow in coming to the Western churches, it
is now obligatory in the Roman Church, for the very reason
that only in this way can the priest (whether consciously or
unconsciously) attain full identification with both Christ and
the Virgin Mother without the guilt of incest.[3] In the male-
oriented culture of the East, where the Virgin is not the
dominant symbol, celibacy is not so essential, and hence
not obligatory.

Symbols

Perhaps one of the most difficult tasks for a Protestant
in Latin America is to realize the nature and importance of
symbols, whether verbal or visual. This does not mean that
Protestants do not possess a number of symbols; they do.
But for the most part Protestant symbols are words and
verbal descriptions of people and events. When the Protestant thinks of Saint Peter, a whole series of images
immediately comes to the surface of his thinking. These
images include the denial at the trial, the three questions
posed by Jesus after the resurrection, Peter cutting off

Malchus' ear, etc. For the average Roman Catholic in Latin America, Saint Peter means a statue in a particular church, a patron saint of a nearby town, a statue before which he prays in times of sickness in the family, a personage in heaven who intercedes with Mary, who in turn goes to Christ. If a Roman Catholic happens to have read the Bible, he may have some mental images similar to those of the Protestant, but even if the Protestant and the Catholic use the same words "Saint Peter," they are very likely to be thinking about quite different referents.

A number of Protestant symbols are words for beliefs, many of which the average Protestant cannot explain. These words symbolize important experiences in his life and doctrines which he believes are indispensable to faith: repentance, conversion, redemption, blessing, Holy Spirit, justification, sanctification, the dying Savior, the blood, the cross, the open tomb, confession, prayer, faith, hope, assurance, etc. For the Roman Catholic a number of these words are associated with specific objects (or images) which he can see or rites in which he overtly participates: the blood (the wine at communion or red paint on the crucifix), the dying Savior (the crucifix), the cross, saints (heavenly intercessors and images within the home and at church), prayers, faith (as a list of doctrines), confession (to the priest), etc. However, for a number of word symbols which the average Protestant possesses there is often no corresponding object or mental image for the Catholic. For the most part, Roman Catholicism has objectified its symbols in attractive or awesome objects or in impressive rites, while the Protestant emphasizes much more the abstract of historical value of the word symbols.

Biblical symbolization

Roman Catholic leaders who have been influenced by the movement for biblical renewal within the Church have become increasingly concerned because so many traditional symbols of the ritual are relatively meaningless to the people, even though they may be emotionally attractive. As a corrective to overemphasis upon visual symbols and ritual acts, many Roman Catholic priests have introduced radical departures in liturgy and in preaching. The Bible, the cross, and the

empty tomb are all being reemphasized. The rent veil
becomes a symbol of man's acceptance by God through the
work of Christ. The mass takes on more and more the
symbolic meaning of the covenant meal, consecrated by the
death of the one who offered himself to validate the covenant.
And the risen Lord transforms the crucifix into an empty
cross, to give assurance that "death is swallowed up in
victory."

One of the reasons for the spectacular success of Pentecostal churches in many parts of Latin America is their
rich use of symbols. Most of these are verbal, but they are
reinforced by dynamic group participation, rich colors (for
both the interior and exterior of churches), and dramatic
preaching, in which the preacher plays the role of the actor
and the congregation participates as the chorus—closely
parallel to ancient dramas.

Both Roman Catholics and Protestants are becoming
increasingly sensitive to the power and influence of symbols
—tools by which the mind creates either edifices of worship
or prisons of illusion. No people can be understood without
an appreciation of their symbols and a knowledge of the
factors which have produced the symbols. But to understand
the symbols is only the first step; the symbols must be
used to communicate, to comprehend, and to enrich the
whole of life.

8

The Indigenous Churches in Latin America[1]

Protestant churches in Latin America are of four basic types: (1) mission-directed churches, which make no pretense to being indigenous or under local leadership, (2) "national-front" churches, which are really mission-directed, but which make use of local persons for leadership, (3) "indigenized" churches, in which missions have previously had control but which are now being managed by national leaders in various countries, though often with direct financial support and indirect "leverage" on policy and programming, and (4) fully indigenous churches, in the sense that they have developed exclusively with Latin leadership and funds.[2]

In most instances these indigenous churches owe much to missionary endeavor, for they are in some cases an early breakoff from formal missionary work. This is true of the Pentecostal work in Chile, which began in 1909, when a Methodist missionary left the mission and started the Pentecostal work in that land. In other instances, the independent churches may be one "spiritual generation" removed from missionary influence, as when the Pentecostal work in Argentina takes much of its inspiration from leaders in Chile or when a group of Otomí Indians in the Mesquital area of Mexico is reached through a strong Otomí leader who has had contact with a local church in Pachuca, which in turn is the result of some early missionary endeavor of a British mining engineer some years before.

Approaches to the study of the indigenous churches

A study of the various indigenous churches in Latin America could be carried out along three significant lines: (1) statistical, (2) historical, and (3) structural. Unfortunately, we do not have adequate statistics about such movements, and in many instances there is little available historical information. Gathering statistics on such groups is quite difficult, for there are often no central organizations or control, and most groups are quite unconcerned with statistics. Moreover, most of these groups are growing dynamically and they are, relatively speaking, so recent that the people have not sensed the need for any history of their movements. People rarely become interested in writing history while they are making it; and these groups, with their dynamic outward thrust, are making history so fast that they do not sense the need for tracing their own developments.

We can, however, study these movements structurally, since there are a number of distinctive features which reveal some striking relationships to the cultural backgrounds of the people. Moreover, since these structures have grown up with the people (they are the only ones the people have known), they have an indigenous legitimacy and strength which many imported structures simply do not have. It is for this reason that in so many respects these groups are outdistancing other more highly subsidized, better educated, and historically recognized groups.

Pentecostal tendencies in the indigenous churches

It would be entirely wrong to classify all the indigenous churches in Latin America as being "Pentecostal" in the usual sense of this word. In fact, there are great differences between some of the extreme emotional excesses of certain Chilean congregations and the more reserved fervor of a congregation such as the one at Portales in Mexico City. Moreover, even within a single movement there are wide differences of practice. On the other hand, certain significant features are broadly characteristic of most of these indigenous groups: (1) emphasis on divine healing (often to the extent of regarding the use of medicines as evidence of weakness of faith), (2) belief in speaking in tongues (though some groups insist on interpretation for any occurrence of tongues and hence tend to make such demonstrations more orderly and controlled), (3) belief in filling of the Spirit (as evidenced by healing or the gift of tongues), (4) deep emotional fervor, often exhibited in dancing, shouting, and crying, (5) general adherence to a kind of "holiness doctrine" characteristic of certain forms of Wesleyanism, (6) importance of prayer and the receiving of answers to prayer (prayer is generally engaged in by all the congregation, orally and simultaneously), and (7) a type of literal biblicism which takes the Bible seriously and uncritically.

It is difficult to classify these movements as simply "Pentecostal." Actually, there are so many types that one must often say "Pentecostal-like." But there are no more extreme types in Latin America than exist within this same general kind of movement in the United States.

These indigenous churches also differ widely in their basic structures and functioning. However, in this area also, there are some important structural features which tend to characterize these many formally unrelated movements.

Development of a ministry through apprenticeship

The leadership of the various indigenous movements in Latin America tends to be "laymen" who have worked their way up in the churches through an informal kind of apprenticeship system. They often begin as young men ushering in the church, then selling Scriptures or tracts. This may be followed by a period as Sunday school teachers, then as deacons or elders, and finally as assistant pastors, often in small, newly formed congregations. Finally, when these persons are forty or fifty years of age, they may become full pastors of a church. Even with full ministerial responsibilities for a large congregation they may continue to earn a living at some secular job, while giving all their spare time to the church. In other cases they may become full-time workers for the church, but in most cases this is only after they have reached maturity. The obvious advantage of this type of program is that neophytes are not turned loose on congregations before they are seasoned by experience in a number of roles in church life. Moreover, by the selective process only those with real leadership ability tend to rise to the top.

This informal apprenticeship system was not worked out by any special design. It is actually the only system the people have known, for this is precisely the manner in which many local persons ultimately became Roman Catholic priests: first they were choirboys, then catechists and sacristans; finally they were ordained. Moreover, these Pentecostal movements generally have had no funds to set up Bible schools and certainly no money to pay the salaries of the graduates. But in the process they have solved two nagging problems: (1) how to support a ministry (the ministers supported themselves until they were capable of attracting a church with sufficient members to support them) and (2) how to select capable persons. Rather than basing a system on a missionary's choice, this program has evolved a spiritual "survival of the fittest," which has resulted in the development of leadership rather than "followership" (the normal result of paternalistic supervision).

A functional class structure

The indigenous model used for the development of these churches in Latin America has been the local Indian or small town social structure, which represents a number of important class distinctions, with each one based essentially on varying grades of responsibility. In a well-organized Roman Catholic small town in Latin America, the people are highly organized for the various responsibilities in the church. Some groups are responsible for clothing the saints, others for organizing the fiestas, while still other groups may be given the tasks of keeping the church clean, providing food for the priests, or working on the lands of the church. Heading up such a structure are the Roman Catholic priest and the elders of the town, who constitute a kind of self-perpetuating leadership. This leadership group controls the assigning of tasks and the raising of people from one grade to another.

The indigenous churches of Latin America exhibit very similar structures, in which almost everyone is given work to do. In the Portales Church in Mexico City, for example, new converts are put under the special charge of "older brothers or sisters in the faith," who are to guide the spiritual lives of the new members. Others are given the job of evangelizing, calling on new families, and inviting people to church. Many assume responsibility for one of the prayer vigils, for the church is kept open for groups praying 24 hours a day, every day of the year. Still others receive money from the church as a means of beginning their "talents," and as they buy and sell with this money, they turn in the proceeds to the church—a source of an incredibly large income from a relatively poor congregation. Many of the better-educated persons may assume responsibility for a teaching ministry, for praying for the sick, for organizing churches in other areas of the city, or for making trips out into the country where persons who have visited the city church extend invitations for someone to come with the Good News to the more remote towns.

At the top of this structure is either a group of men or a single strong personality who dominates the group. The strength of this structure is, however, (1) the full participation of almost everyone and (2) a gradation which depends largely on function rather than background. Since the people come so largely from the same general socioeconomic class, there is not the same tendency for the rich or well-educated to stifle the development of the more humble people as is the case in many churches of the more historical denominations.

Effective adaptation to local circumstances

Having arisen out of the environment of which they are a part, these movements are really indigenous. That is to say, they fit, or they just would not have come into existence. These movements differ considerably from place to place. The patterns of life in the slums of Mexico City are, for example, very different from those in the rural Mesquital region to the north. In the latter, a group of about 2,500 Otomí Indians have worked out a very remarkable adaptation to most difficult socioeconomic problems. This region has been desperately poor and violently fanatical. As a result of having accepted the gospel, the first Otomí converts in the area were dispossessed of their lands and driven away. They finally managed to purchase a barren, neglected hill not far from the highway, where they built modest homes and set up a Christian community. They largely shared their resources, taught each other local skills, and built their houses and chapels with cooperative labor. As the community grew, they began to cooperate with the government in road-building projects when other local groups refused. As their leader explained, the people believed in "the redemption of their hands by work, of their minds by learning to read, of their bodies through divine healing, and of their souls by the new birth from above."

This group has no formal system of instruction for the teaching of people. Rather, they invite any new convert to come and live in the community for six months to a year, during which time he learns what it means to be a Christian. He participates in almost daily religious services, learns to pray by praying, learns to trust God through the joint devotion and trials of the community, and finally is sent back to his own town or to another, where he becomes a member of one of the 30 or so congregations meeting in various chapels throughout the region.

In contrast with this highly organized but "low-pressure" type of social structure, with its strong emphasis upon economic development and personal responsibility, the Pentecostal development among the Toba Indians of northern Argentina[3] is an instructive example of quite another type of adaptation. There, in the region near Sáenz Peña, some Pentecostal leaders contacted a number of Indians who, after a crushing defeat by the Argentine army, finally decided to do an about-face and "join the white man."

Some Mennonite missionaries who had been in the area for some time had been quite unsuccessful in making important contacts with these Tobas. The Mennonite orientation was toward economic responsibility and individual resourcefulness and the seminomadic Tobas could not understand this kind of "save and slave" way of life. They had so long been immersed in a kind of "vulture culture," in which it was either feast or famine, that they felt a person's only security rested in the solidarity of the group, not in the resourcefulness of the individual. In their period of disillusionment, however, the Pentecostal message had

tremendous appeal. Whereas before only certain persons
could be medicine men and enjoy ecstatic experiences of
fellowship with the ancestral spirits, as Pentecostals all
people could be possessed by the Spirit of God and could
enjoy the thrill of this new religious ecstasy. Moreover,
this message of God's redeeming grace was explained as a
way in which God "shared" his Son with men and his Son
"shares" his Spirit. This theme of sharing struck a respon-
sive chord, for willingness to share is a basic feature in
Toba life.

Within a few years some 10,000 Tobas, out of a tribe
numbering about 15,000, became Evangelicals. Of course,
their understanding of the Christian message was not very
deep, but their loyalty to Jesus Christ has been strong.
Accordingly, the Mennonite missionaries are now wisely not
trying to make Mennonites of the people but are working out
ways whereby these people may be served where they are.

A relevant message

It is all too easy to make a hasty judgment of a typical
sermon in these indigenous churches and to conclude that
the topic and presentation is superficial and marginal to the
truth of Christianity. A more careful analysis will often
reveal something far more relevant than may have appeared
at first. For example, in the Portales Church on Reformation
Day in 1959, there was no mention of Luther; in fact, the
Reformation as such was not even the topic of the day.
Rather, as this was the Sunday before All Saints' Day, the
theme of both the Sunday school and church service was:
What is still pagan in our beliefs and customs on All Saints'
Day? Rather than studying the Reformation which occurred
centuries ago, these people were vitally concerned with how
they could produce a reformation in their own lives and
community, as they witnessed to their friends and neighbors.

An emphasis on divine healing is sometimes regarded by
outsiders as a dangerous fad, but when one realizes that in
Latin America there is such a preoccupation with psychosomatic disease, especially the "evil eye" and the *susto*
"fright" or "shock," it is no wonder that a gospel of healing
has such relevance. Even in Roman Catholicism, much of
the focus of attention on the saints is related to healing, and

it is not strange that this same concern should carry over into Protestant communities.

Effective means of communication

Some Pentecostal-type sermons in Latin America are theologically thin, but often they are more effectively directed to the needs of the people than many sermons delivered in more traditional churches. It is true that these indigenous churches seldom engage in comprehensive Bible study. Moreover, one seldom hears a series of messages on a particular section of the Bible, for the ministers are generally not concerned with teaching the Bible but with teaching the people. Their ministry is person-centered, but they do proclaim the *kerygma*. They consistently and repeatedly emphasize certain key points: (1) the plan and purpose of God as revealed in the death and resurrection of Jesus Christ, (2) the need to repent and be baptized, and (3) the necessity of becoming a part of the church as a witnessing member.

The real communication that takes place within one of these indigenous churches is often not centered in the sermon, as important as that may seem superficially. More is communicated by group participation in prayer, by the concentrated attention of the people on the ritual (which, though informal, is highly organized), and by a kind of folk drama (this is essentially what one finds in many of these churches). In many churches the pastors customarily build their sermons around biblical heroes. On a typical occasion in Santiago, Chile, the pastor selected Zacchaeus, whom he described first as an embittered man who sought revenge against his own people by becoming a tax collector. Nevertheless he was a person with an empty heart and one supreme desire: to see Jesus. Then the pastor turned to the congregation and asked, "How many of you this day want to see Jesus?" Immediately, the entire congregation fell to their knees, crying to the Lord. Within a few minutes the congregation ceased praying, and the pastor continued with the "second act" in the drama: he described how Zacchaeus in his desire to see Jesus ran ahead of the crowd and climbed a tree, and just at the most crucial time he not only saw Jesus, but Jesus saw him and called him by name. The pastor again turned to the people and asked how many had been called by Jesus. A second time the congregation fell to their knees, but this time the psychological atmosphere of the praying was entirely different. Then the pastor explained to the people that if they were to enjoy the presence of the Lord in their hearts they must be willing to make retribution for their sins, even as Zacchaeus had done, and again he challenged them to take this step if they were to have the Lord within their hearts. And again the people knelt, and this time the atmosphere was still different.

This type of religious drama is strikingly similar to what existed in ancient Greece, in which there was only one actor and the chorus. In this church in Santiago the preacher was the actor and the entire congregation the chorus. The power of this type of preaching is that it provides a means of psychological identification and participation which cannot be equaled in the services of the more traditional and dignified denominations.

Emphasis on worship

While many churches in Latin America seem more like classrooms than places of worship, the indigenous churches emphasize the importance of worship as communication with God.[4] They are not so concerned with communication *about* God but with a relation *to* God, through prayer to Him and listening to His voice in ecstatic devotion.

In many of the more formal churches a person may attend for years without ever learning how to pray, since prayer is so often regarded as a semiprofessional accomplishment, with only certain persons taking the lead. In these indigenous churches, however, everyone prays, and the contagion is such that one can scarcely avoid praying. Certainly, the noise of others praying reduces the newcomer's timidity. Mistakes in grammar, diction, or even sentiment can scarcely be heard, even by one's closest neighbor.

Despite all the "hubbub" which seems to characterize the Pentecostal-type meeting, there is nevertheless a great deal of genuine feeling of the presence of God and a sense of group participation which is the life blood of a congregation.

Dangers in the indigenous movements in Latin America

No appraisal of the indigenous movements in Latin America can be justly made without a realistic understanding of some of the dangers, for these do exist. For one thing there is a tendency toward *caudillismo* "strong leadership," which can degenerate into irresponsible leadership or "bossism." These strong leaders sometimes demand the kind of blind devotion with which the people may have been formerly familiar in the Roman Church. However, the dangers in this type of dominating personalism are not much greater than what one finds in other churches where a tradition of mission paternalism has produced severe tensions and enervating resentments.

At the same time one must recognize that there is a tendency for many of the Pentecostal pastors to emphasize too exclusively the emotional and exhortatory aspects of their message, so that as a result they fail to "feed the flock." The people may be emotionally "whipped" Sunday after Sunday, and only those who can stand such psychological flagellation come out spiritually alive. The others tend to fall along the way. However, it is encouraging that in some instances pastors are themselves coming to recognize more and more the need of Bible study. Moreover, the people in these indigenous churches not only buy Bibles in great quantities, but they make constant use of such books. In fact, some of these churches could be very appropriately known as the "churches of the dirty Bibles," since the people read their Bibles assiduously, often with dirty fingers, tracing out line after line of the text.

A third danger, and perhaps the greatest, is the isolation that such groups have from the rest of the Christian community. They are, of course, not easy to reach, since they are basically suspicious of any overtures from people of the more traditional churches. They sense that in many instances they come from a different socioeconomic class, and this only tends to strengthen their theologically founded suspicion that other Evangelicals look down on them. On the other hand, the experience of agents of the Bible Society, who have some of the widest contacts with these various groups, is that the people in the indigenous movement are often quite desirous of recognition. They want to be accepted for what they are and not for what others would like to have them be.

A certain amount of rapport is developing between some of these indigenous groups and certain of the faith missions in Latin America, and in some cases leaders of certain Pentecostal groups in the United States have endeavored to work out a fraternal relationship with kindred groups in Latin America. Actually there is much to learn from such people and much to be gained, since in many important respects these are the people who have solved some of the most basic problems of relevant communication and effective organization. Moreover, with the increasing importance of the "mass man" in Latin America, which focuses more and more vital attention on the proletariat, these churches will increasingly be in the center of meaningful political, economic, and social revolution.

Effective understanding and cooperation
with indigenous movements

The real problem of fuller fellowship is the reluctance of many persons in the more traditional movements to associate with people who are unconsciously classed as socially inferior and outwardly rejected as being doctrinally less pure. Actually, the issue of doctrines, though it has some relevance, is not as basic as it might seem, since in some of the fundamental doctrines of the Scriptures indigenous churches have shown amazing insight. With respect to the doctrine of the church, they tend to live out what others only theorize about. The emphasis on social solidarity, mutual help, and belonging makes of their church a congregation rather than merely a building. In their doctrine of redemption, they likewise have an important focal element: that God is love. It is not without significance that in many of these churches the words placed over the altar are *Dios es amor* "God is love." Such churches do not pay much attention to some of the more technical aspects of redemption, such as the particular substitutionary nature of the atonement, but they do emphasize the personal relation of God to man, and it is this redeeming encounter that transforms the lives of thousands.

Perhaps one of the most important doctrines in many of

these indigenous churches is Christian responsibility. This is conveyed largely through the system of full participation and ordered functions.

These indigenous movements have not "arrived." If they had, they would perhaps already be showing the signs of institutional decay. They are only beginning. But even though they do run the risk of becoming in some instances "cults of the Holy Spirit," they are nevertheless in many respects in the same line of tradition which won the followers of George Fox the name of Quakers and resulted in the Methodists being forced out of the more dignified places of worship because of their emotional ways. One can only thank God that these churches have been able to reach so many of the economically and socially dispossessed, and have become the "third force" of religion in Latin America.

Notes

Part I

NOTES on Chapter 1
SIMILARITIES AND CONTRASTS

1   John P. Gillin, "Some Signposts for Policy," in Lyman
    Bryson, ed., SOCIAL CHANGE IN LATIN AMERICA
    TODAY (New York: Random House, 1960), pp. 48 ff.
2   Lyman Bryson, ed., SOCIAL CHANGE IN LATIN
    AMERICA TODAY (New York: Random House, 1960),
    p. 3.
3   Gillin, op. cit., p. 20.
4   Ibid., p. 26.
5   Bryson, op. cit., has compiled a very similar listing:
    personal dignity, family cohesion, social hierarchy,
    spiritual fatalism, propriety and decency in the way of
    life, and scorn of manual labor.
6   Samuel Ramos, EL PERFIL DEL HOMBRE Y LA
    CULTURA EN MEXICO (Buenos Aires and Mexico
    City: Espasa-Calpe Argentina, 1951), pp. 58 ff.
7   María Elvira Bermúdez, LA VIDA FAMILIAR DEL
    MEXICANO (Mexico City: Antigua Librería Robredo,
    1955), pp. 97 ff.
8   Rogelio Díaz Guerrero, ESTUDIOS DE PSICOLOGIA
    DEL MEXICANO (Mexico City: Antigua Librería
    Robredo, 1961), pp. 12 ff.
9   This largely traditional interpretation of Sancho Panza
    does have a certain validity, but it is important to
    realize that this may also be a very simplistic and
    perhaps even wrong interpretation of the role of Sancho,
    who embodies a good deal of idealism and as the story
    progresses shows increasing quijotismo.
10 Miguel de Unamuno, OBRAS SELECTAS (Madrid:
    Editorial Plenitud, 1956), p. 87.
11 Octavio Paz, EL LABERINTO DE LA SOLEDAD
    (segunda ed., Mexico City: Fondo de Cultura Eco-
    nómica, 1959), pp. 21-22.
12 Ramos, op. cit., pp. 33-34.
13 Luis Quintanilla, A LATIN AMERICAN SPEAKS (New
    York: Macmillan, 1943), p. 16.
14 Ramos, op. cit., p. 69.

NOTES on Chapter 2
AUTHORITARIANISM AND INDIVIDUALISM

1   Bermúdez, op. cit., p. 115.
2   Gillin, op. cit., p. 53.
3   Santiago Ramírez, EL MEXICANO: PSICOLOGIA
    DE SUS MOTIVACIONES (Mexico City: Editorial
    Pax-México, 1959), p. 37.
4   Ramos, op. cit., p. 18.
5   Unamuno, op. cit., p. 105.
6   See Unamuno's literary analysis of Don Quijote, ibid.,
    pp. 259-496.
7   Gonzalo Báez-Camargo, LA NOTA EVANGELICA EN
    LA POESIA HISPANO-AMERICANA (Mexico City:
    Ediciones Luminar, 1960), p. 7.
8   Ibid., pp. 10-12. Though there were certain signifi-
    cant religious literary developments in Spain, these
    never took root to any extent in Latin America. The
    precise reasons for this are difficult to determine.
9   Unamuno, op. cit., p. 108.
10 Báez-Camargo, op. cit., pp. 8-10.
11 Gillin, op. cit., pp. 34-45.
12 Ibid., p. 32.
13 Paz, op. cit., p. 22.
14 Gillin, op. cit., p. 22.
15 Bryson, op. cit., p. 8.
16 Paz, op. cit., pp. 32, 43, 45.
17 Ibid., p. 46.
18 Ibid., p. 47.
19 Unamuno, op. cit., p. 101.
20 Rogelio Díaz Guerrero, op. cit., p. 62.
21 Paz, op. cit., pp. 38-39.
22 Bryson, op. cit., p. 7.

NOTES on Chapter 3
IDEALISM AND REALISM

1   Abelardo Villegas, LA FILOSOFIA DE LO MEXI-
    CANO (Mexico City: Fondo de Cultura Económica,
    1960), p. 33.
2   Unamuno, op. cit., p. 88.
3   Villegas, op. cit., pp. 33 ff.

4   Paz, op. cit., pp. 110-111.
5   Ibid., p. 21.
6   John Mackay, EL SENTIDO DE LA VIDA, p. 267.
7   Unamuno, op. cit., p. 91.
8   Ramos, op. cit., p. 85.
9   Ramírez, op. cit., pp. 57-58.
10 Mackay, op. cit., p. 4.
11 Villegas, op. cit., p. 70.
12 Ibid., p. 112.
13 Ramírez, op. cit., p. 120.
14 Ramos, op. cit., p. 16.
15 Ibid., p. 119.
16 Ibid., pp. 38-39.
17 Villegas, op. cit., p. 87.
18 Díaz, op. cit., pp. 31-32.
19 Bermúdez, op. cit., p. 60.
20 Ibid., p. 56.

NOTES on Chapter 4
MACHISMO AND HEMBRISMO

1   Ramírez, op. cit., p. 48.
2   Villegas, op. cit., p. 126.
3   Ramírez, op. cit., pp. 61 ff.
4   Paz, op. cit., p. 72.
5   Bermúdez, op. cit., p. 84.
6   Díaz, op. cit., pp. 14, 18.
7   Aniceto Aramoni, PSICOANALISIS DE LA DINA-
    MICA DE UN PUEBLO (Mexico City: Universidad
    Nacional Autonóma de México, 1961), p. 244.
8   Ibid., p. 219.
9   Díaz, op. cit., p. 21.
10 Ibid., p. 48.
11 One may well find that psychosomatic illnesses in
    North America are equally prevalent, but the causes
    are generally attributed to quite different causes, e.g.
    social climbing, job insecurity, a success syndrome,
    and emotional abandonment in childhood.
12 Villegas, op. cit., p. 125; Ramos, op. cit., pp. 53-54.
13 Aramoni, op. cit., p. 125.
14 Díaz, op. cit., p. 58.
15 Bermúdez, op. cit., p. 55.

16   Ibid., p. 42.
17   These categories are not mutually exclusive.
18   Mackay, op. cit., pp. 5 ff.
19   Bermúdez, op. cit., p. 85.
20   Aramoni, op. cit., p. 149.
21   Ibid., p. 277.
22   Paz, op. cit., p. 35.
23   Bermúdez, op. cit., p. 52.
24   Aramoni, op. cit., pp. 203-204.
25   Paz, op. cit., p. 37.
26   Bermúdez, op. cit., pp. 53 ff.
27   Ibid., p. 71.
28   Mackay, op. cit., p. 5.
29   Ramírez, op. cit., pp. 129-130.
30   Ibid., p. 85.
31   Paz, op. cit., pp. 73-74.
32   Bermúdez, op. cit., p. 85.
33   Ramírez, op. cit., pp. 92 ff.

Part II

NOTES on Chapter 5
SOCIAL STRUCTURE AND EVANGELISM

1   Reprinted from PRACTICAL ANTHROPOLOGY, vol.
     5 (1958), pp. 101-123.

NOTES on Chapter 6
CHRISTO-PAGANISM

1   Reprinted from PRACTICAL ANTHROPOLOGY, vol.
     8 (1961), p. 1-15.
2   See William L. Wonderly, "Pagan and Christian
     Concepts in a Mexican Indian Culture," PRACTICAL
     ANTHROPOLOGY, vol. 5, (1958), pp. 197-202.

NOTES on Chapter 7
MARIOLOGY IN LATIN AMERICA

1   Reprinted from PRACTICAL ANTHROPOLOGY, vol.
     4 (1957), pp. 69-82.
2   Masochistic individuals are of course the exceptions to
     this general scheme, and it is not without significance

that some of the more rigorous orders of the Roman Church have been characterized by masochistic rites, centering in identification with the crucified Christ.
3   It is quite true that these explanations involve several important features of Freudian psychology, but they are by no means dependent solely upon an acceptance or rejection of Freudian theories. These fundamental psychological relationships are recognized in one form or another by practically all psychoanalysts.

NOTES on Chapter 8
THE INDIGENOUS CHURCHES IN LATIN AMERICA

1   Reprinted from PRACTICAL ANTHROPOLOGY, vol. 8 (1961), pp. 97-105.
2   See William A. Smalley, "Cultural Implications of an Indigenous Church," PRACTICAL ANTHROPOLOGY, vol. 5 (1958), pp. 53-65.
3   William D. Reyburn, TOBA INDIANS OF THE ARGENTINE CHACO, AN INTERPRETIVE REPORT, (Elkhart, Indiana: Mennonite Board of Missions and Charities, 1954).
4   See Eugene A. Nida, RELIGION ACROSS CULTURES (New York: Harper and Row, 1968).

Glossary

aguardiente - corn liquor
aires - "winds", spirit forces

brujo - sorcerer, witch doctor

caudillo - head, chief, leader
civilizado - civilized
comadre - godmother
compadre - godfather
compadrazgo - godfather relationship
copal - incense used in ceremonial practices
costumbres - customs, way of life
criollo - person born in Latin America of European, usually Spanish, descent
curandero - healer, medical person, usually working in rural areas, and usually not professionally trained

dueño - owner
Dios Mundo - "God of the world"

ermita - local shrine
espiritualidad - quality of having spiritual values

fiesta - local village-wide celebration

gente decente - respectable people, civilized
guitarrón - large guitar-like instrument

hembrismo - female dependence, passivity and receptivity
hombridad - masculinity

ladino - person of Latin (Spanish) culture, though may be of mixed Indian and Spanish blood

macho - masculine
machismo - male dominance, sexuality, authoritarianism and display
mentira - lie
mestizo - person of mixed blood of white and Indian
mayordomo - overseer, foreman
muy macho - very masculine, displaying male qualities of leadership and dominance

palanca - lever, influence
pandilla - gang of young boys
paterfamilias - dominant figure
patrón - landlord, boss, sponsor
patroncito - familiar form of landlord, sponsor
pecado - sin
pecadillos - little sins
peón - laborer
personalismo - individualism

quijotismo - romantic idealism

sanchismo - earthy and materialistic concern for immediate physical gratification

Bibliography

Adams, Richard N., "Cultural Components of Central America," AMERICAN ANTHROPOLOGIST, 58 (1956), 881-907.

Adorno, T. W., et al., THE AUTHORITARIAN PERSONALITY. New York: Harper and Brothers, 1950.

Aramoni, Aniceto, PSICOANALISIS DE LA DINAMICA DE UN PUEBLO. Mexico City: Universidad Nacional Autónoma de México, 1961.

Arciniegas, German, ed., THE GREEN CONTINENT. New York: Alfred A. Knopf, 1944.

Báez-Camargo, Gonzalo, LA NOTA EVANGELICA EN LA POESIA HISPANO-AMERICANA. Mexico City: Ediciones Luminar, 1960.

Bermúdez, Maria Elvira, LA VIDA FAMILIAR DEL MEXICANO. Mexico City: Antigua Librería Robredo, 1955.

Blanksten, George I., ECUADOR: CONSTITUTIONS AND CAUDILLOS. Berkeley: University of California Press, 1951.

Bryson, Lyman, ed., SOCIAL CHANGE IN LATIN AMERICA TODAY. New York: Random House, 1960.

Bunge, Carlos Octavio, NUESTRA AMERICA: ENSAYO DE PSICOLOGIA SOCIAL. Buenos Aires: Administración General, 1918.

Cantril, M., GAUGING PUBLIC OPINION. Princeton: Princeton University Press, 1944.

Caso, Antonio, EL PUEBLO DEL SOL. Mexico City: Fondo de Cultura Económica, 1953.

Cline, Howard F., THE UNITED STATES AND MEXICO. Cambridge: Harvard University Press, 1953.

Crevenna, Theo. R., ed., MATERIALES PARA EL ESTUDIO DE LA CLASE MEDIA EN LA AMERICA LATINA. Washington: Pan American Union, 1950-51.

Díaz Guerrero, Rogelio, ESTUDIOS DE PSICOLOGIA DEL MEXICANO. Antigua Libería Robredo, 1961.

Dollard, John, et al., FRUSTRATION AND AGGRESSION. New Haven: Yale University Press, 1943.

Duran Ochoa, J., POBLACION. Mexico City: Fondo de Cultura Económica, 1955.

Foster, George, A CROSS CULTURAL ANTHROPOLOGICAL ANALYSIS OF A TECHNICAL AID PROGRAM. Washington: Smithsonian Institution, 1951.

Fromm, Eric, MAN FOR HIMSELF. New York: Rine-
    hart and Co., 1947.
Gallegos, Rómulo, DOÑA BARBARA. Buenos Aires:
    Espasa-Calpe Argentina (Colección Austral), 1941.
    (First edition, 1929.)
Germani, Gino, ESTRUCTURA SOCIAL DE LA ARGEN-
    TINA. Buenos Aires: Editorial Raigal, 1955.
Gillin, John, and K. H. Silvert, "Ambiguities in Guatemala,"
    FOREIGN AFFAIRS. New York, 1956, pp. 469-482.
Gillin, John P., "Some Signposts for Policy," in Lyman
    Bryson, ed., SOCIAL CHANGE IN LATIN AMERICA
    TODAY. New York: Random House, 1960, pp. 14-62.
González Pineda, F., EL MEXICANO: SU DINAMICA
    PSICOSOCIAL. Mexico City: Editorial Pax-México,
    1959.
Hall, Robert A., Jr., CULTURAL SYMBOLISM IN LIT-
    ERATURE. Ithaca, N. Y.: Linguistica, 1963.
Holmberg, Allan R., "Changing Community Attitudes and
    Values in Peru," in Lyman Bryson, ed., SOCIAL
    CHANGE IN LATIN AMERICA TODAY. New York:
    Random House, 1960, pp. 63-107.
Iturriaga, José E., LA ESTRUCTURA SOCIAL Y CUL-
    TURAL DE MEXICO. Mexico City: Fondo de Cul-
    tura Económica, 1951.
Johnson, John J., POLITICAL CHANGE IN LATIN
    AMERICA: THE EMERGENCE OF THE MIDDLE
    SECTORS. Palo Alto: Stanford University Press,
    1958.
Lewis, Oscar, FIVE FAMILIES. New York: Basic Books,
    1959.
Lewis, Oscar, "Mexico Since Cardenas," in Lyman
    Bryson, ed., SOCIAL CHANGE IN LATIN AMERICA
    TODAY. New York: Random House, 1960, pp. 285-345.
Luria, A. R., NATURE OF HUMAN CONFLICTS. New
    York: Liveright, 1932.
Mackay, John A., THE OTHER SPANISH CHRIST. New
    York: Macmillan, 1932.
Mackay, John A., EL SENTIDO DE LA VIDA. Buenos
    Aires: Editorial La Aurora, 1932.
Mosk, Sanford A., "Indigenous Economy in Latin America."
    INTER-AMERICAN ECONOMIC AFFAIRS, Washington,
    D. C., 1954, pp. 3-25.

Mosk, Sanford A., THE INDUSTRIAL REVOLUTION IN MEXICO. Berkeley: University of California, 1950.

Nida, Eugene A., CUSTOMS AND CULTURES. New York: Harper and Brothers, 1954.

Nida, Eugene A., "Kerygma and Culture: Underlying Problems in the Communication of the Gospel in Spanish-Speaking Latin America," LUTHERAN WORLD, 8 (1961), 269-280.

Nida, Eugene A., MESSAGE AND MISSION. New York: Harper and Brothers, 1960.

Nida, Eugene A., "Religion: Communication with the Supernatural," PRACTICAL ANTHROPOLOGY, 7 (May-June, 1960), 97-112.

Nida, Eugene A., "The Role of Language in Contemporary Africa," PRACTICAL ANTHROPOLOGY, 4 (July-August, 1957), 136.

Nida, Eugene A., RELIGION ACROSS CULTURES. New York: Harper and Row, 1968.

Northrop, F. S. C., THE MEETING OF EAST AND WEST. New York: Macmillan, 1946.

Parra, Manuel German, LA INDUSTRIALIZACION DE MEXICO. Mexico City: Imprenta Universitaria, 1954.

Patch, Richard W., "Bolivia: U. S. Assistance in a Revolutionary Setting," in Lyman Bryson, ed., SOCIAL CHANGE IN LATIN AMERICA TODAY. New York: Random House, 1960, pp. 108-175.

Paz, Octavio, EL LABERINTO DE LA SOLEDAD. Mexico City: Fondo de Cultura Económica, 1959 (segunda edición).

Quintanilla, Luis, A LATIN AMERICAN SPEAKS. New York: Macmillan, 1943.

Ramírez, Santiago, EL MEXICANO: PSICOLOGIA DE SUS MOTIVACIONES. Mexico City: Editorial Paz-México, 1959.

Ramos, Samuel, EL PERFIL DEL HOMBRE Y LA CULTURA EN MEXICO. Buenos Aires and Mexico City: Espasa-Calpe Argentina, 1951.

Reed, A., OROZCO. Mexico City: Fondo de Cultura Económica, 1955.

Reulet, Anibal Sánchez, ed., LA FILOSOFIA LATINO-AMERICANA CONTEMPORANEA. Washington: Pan American Union, 1949.

Reyburn, Wm. D., TOBA INDIANS OF THE ARGENTINE CHACO: AN INTERPRETIVE REPORT. Elkhart, Ind.: Mennonite Board of Missions and Charities, 1954.

Rojas, Ricardo, THE INVISIBLE CHRIST, trans. by Webster E. Browning. New York: Abingdon, 1931.

Rycroft, W. Stanley, RELIGION AND FAITH IN LATIN AMERICA. Philadelphia: Westminster, 1958.

Schurz, William Lytle, THIS NEW WORLD: THE CIVILIZATION OF LATIN AMERICA. New York: Dutton and Co., 1954.

Sejourne, L., SUPERVIVENCIAS DE UN MUNDO ANTIGUO. Mexico City: Fondo de Cultura Económica, 1953.

Smalley, William A., "Cultural Implications of an Indigenous Church," PRACTICAL ANTHROPOLOGY, 5 (March-April, 1958), 51-65.

Stagner, Ross, PSYCHOLOGY OF PERSONALITY. New York: McGraw-Hill, 1948.

Tax, Sol, PENNY CAPITALISM: A GUATEMALA INDIAN ECONOMY. Washington: Institute of Social Anthropology, 1953.

Torres-Rioseco, Arturo, THE EPIC OF LATIN AMERICAN LITERATURE. New York: Oxford University Press, 1956.

Unamuno, Miguel de, OBRAS SELECTAS. Madrid: Editorial Plenitud, 1956.

Villegas, Abelardo, LA FILOSOFIA DE LO MEXICANO. Mexico City: Fondo de Cultura Económica, 1960.

Vinueza, Leopoldo Benites, ECUADOR: DRAMA Y PARADOJA. Mexico City: Fondo de Cultura Económica, 1950.

Wagley, Charles, and Marvin Harris, "Typology of Latin American Subcultures," AMERICAN ANTHROPOLOGIST, 57 (1955), 428-451.

Williamson, Rene de Visme, CULTURE AND POLICY: THE UNITED STATES AND THE HISPANIC WORLD. Knoxville: University of Tennessee Press, 1949.

Wonderly, William L., "Pagan and Christian Concepts in a Mexican Indian Culture," PRACTICAL ANTHROPOLOGY, 5 (Sept.-Dec., 1958), 197-202.

Zavala, S., APROXIMACIONES A LA HISTORIA DE MEXICO. Mexico City: Editorial Pourrua y Obregón, 1953.

Index

Dr. Eugene Nida, an Executive Secretary of the American Bible Society, is in charge of the Translations Department and is a foremost linguist and anthropologist. He has travelled extensively throughout the world, but is particularly interested in Latin America since that is where he began his career, working in the early years of its founding with the Wycliffe Bible Translators. He served for a number of years as one of the editors of PRACTICAL ANTHROPOLOGY, and is the author of numerous articles and books on the subjects of linguistics, anthropology, Latin America and missions. His books entitled LEARNING A FOREIGN LANGUAGE, CUSTOMS AND CULTURES, MESSAGE AND MISSION, and GOD'S WORD IN MAN'S LANGUAGE are considered classics in their fields. Although he has written extensively about Latin America, UNDERSTANDING LATIN AMERICANS is his first book size manuscript on that subject.